Pisces Guide to

Venomous & Toxic Marine Life of the World

Patricia Cunningham and Paul Goetz

Pisces Books®
A division of Gulf Publishing Company
Houston, Texas

For our son Michael

Pisces Books®
A division of Gulf Publishing Company
P.O. Box 2608
Houston, Texas 77252-2608

Pisces Books is a registered trademark of Gulf Publishing Company.

Printed in Hong Kong

10   9   8   7   6   5   4   3   2   1

Library of Congress Cataloging-in-Publication Data
Cunningham, Patricia A.
    Pisces guide to venomous and toxic marine life of the world / Patricia A. Cunningham, Paul E. Goetz.
        p.   cm.
    Includes bibliographical references (p.   ) and index.
    ISBN 1-55992-088-2
    1. Marine toxins.   2. Poisonous fishes.   3. Poisonous shellfish. I. Goetz, Paul E.   II. Title.
QP632.M37C86   1996
615.9′4′09162—dc20   —dc20
[615.9′4′09162]   95-34470
                                                            CIP

All photographs by the authors unless otherwise stated. Drawings by Patricia A. Cunningham.

Table of Contents

Juvenile lined catfish often school over coral reefs. Photograph by Carl Roessler.

Acknowledgments

This book is the result of a ten-year effort that has had many starts and stops along the way. Only through encouragement and assistance from family, friends, and many new acquaintances has this project come to fruition. We wish to express our sincerest thanks to everyone involved in this project. Several individuals provided critical assistance at various phases of the project, and to these people, we owe a special thanks.

Dr. G. Yancey Mebane, Associate Director of the Divers Alert Network, Dr. Frank Schwartz of the University of North Carolina Institute of Marine Science, and Paul Humann provided insightful review and comments on an early draft of this book. Longtime friend and technical editor Kathleen Mohar gave us valuable assistance by reviewing the style and language.

We wish to acknowledge all of the photographers whose images greatly enhance the quality of this book. We would especially like to thank Paul Humann, Carl Roessler, and Nancy Sefton who provided not only their photographs, but imparted their experience in the publishing business. The following individuals also gave us assistance in obtaining use of specific photographs or provided us with equipment or facilities: Dr. Bruce Halstead of the World Life Research Institute in Colton, California; Karen Kroslowitz and Regie Kawamoto of the Bishop Museum in Honolulu, Hawaii; Tony Montaner of the Smithsonian Tropical Research Center in Balboa, Panama; Rick Remmert of the Miami Seaquarium in Miami, Florida; and Capt. Jeff Shelnut of Seaquest International in Sunrise, Florida.

A special thanks is also due to our longtime friend and dive buddy Anne Dupont of Delray Beach, Florida, who has provided information, photographs, and encouragement for this project and has graciously provided her spare room for our many trips to Florida.

Last, but most importantly, we thank our young son Michael for his unending patience in allowing us to finish this book.

We have made every attempt to keep the scientific information and photographic identifications of the species profiled in this book as accurate as possible. This was difficult for some species where life history, habitat, and geographic range information varied widely in the scientific literature. Accurate species identification was also complicated, particularly for some of the Indo-Pacific animals, where species characteristics were highly variable.

Foreword

As you read this book, you will learn about the sea creatures that may appear harmless but are capable of wounding, poisoning, or even killing the unlucky diver. Remember, however, that marine animals are generally harmless unless they are deliberately or accidentally threatened or disturbed. Most injuries are the result of a chance encounter (swimming into a jellyfish) or a defensive maneuver (stingray wound) and are rarely due to an aggressive action by the animal.

Research in the management of human injuries from marine animals is still in its infancy, with scarce funding available. The treatments for many types of marine envenomations are largely based on experience and anecdotal reference. Most of the treatments in use have supporters and detractors who engage in heated debate concerning efficacy. The authors recommend a conservative course of action in first aid treatments that is designed to ease the victim's pain, but, at the same time, will not complicate later diagnosis and treatment of the injury by a physician. Much remains to be done to discover effective and reliable treatments based on sound medical research for many types of marine envenomations.

We must not lose sight of the fact that while the effects of venomous and toxic marine creatures on man are important, particularly to the victims, they pale in comparison to the toxic effects human activities have on marine life. Your interest in this guide indicates that you respect the sea and its inhabitants. It is our responsibility to protect, preserve, and share this world of beauty and infinite diversity. Senator Gaylord Nelson of Wisconsin said in 1970 that the environment "is a non-issue in the politics of our country." He led the way in making environmental concerns a public issue by establishing Earth Day, which now has been observed for more than 25 years. There is hope, for we have seen increased public awareness of pollution by industrial chemicals, agricultural pesticides, radioactive materials, and sewage discharged from our cities and rural areas. The public no longer assumes that the oceans have the capacity to absorb infinite quantities of these toxic pollutants. We all must demand that the intentional or accidental dumping of toxic wastes into the ocean by individuals, industry, or government carries severe penalties.

The planet's plight demands an urgent response from each of us. Together we can make a difference in the lives of all creatures, great and small.

G. Yancey Mebane, MD
Associate Director
Divers Alert Network
Duke University Medical Center
Durham, North Carolina

Preface

Most people have had only pleasant encounters with the sea and its inhabitants while diving, snorkeling, swimming, exploring tide pools, or fishing. But there are those who have experienced close encounters of the worst kind with a small number of sea creatures whose contacts with humans are less than pleasant. Like many people who enjoy the ocean, we have our own list of unpleasant encounters. We have been stung by unseen jellyfish, thrown by surge onto sea urchins with foot-long spines, and have unwittingly handled a fire worm. It is not our intent to frighten, but rather to prepare our readers for those rare, but unpleasant encounters that may occur as they enjoy the ocean environment. Our primary purpose in writing this book is to help people avoid painful encounters by learning to recognize venomous and toxic marine animals and to understand their behavior. We researched the recent literature on venomous and toxic marine species and compiled the information into a concise and usable form. Because accidental contacts with some of these animals cannot be avoided, we also provided first aid steps that will reduce the unpleasantness of the contact until professional medical assistance can be obtained. The first aid suggestions represent only immediate steps to reduce pain and the amount of venom that enters the victim. Often, consultation with a physician is required not only in dealing with the toxic effects of the venom, but in treating secondary infections that sometimes develop.

This guide is not an exhaustive account of all venomous and toxic marine life of the world's oceans, but rather it highlights those species that are most commonly encountered or, because of the virulence of their venom, pose the greatest threat to human health. For those who want more information on the range, habitat, or life history of the animals described, a list of references is provided in the bibliography.

Although this book provides specific information on a few of the more commonly encountered species, it can also be of general value in identifying related species of venomous and toxic invertebrates and fish worldwide. The particular species profiled in this book may differ slightly from those in other geographic locations; however, the descriptions provided for recognizing the venomous and toxic animals and recommendations for preventing and treating contacts with them are generally applicable for closely related species.

We hope most readers will use this guide as an aid in identifying venomous and toxic marine species and because of its information will avoid painful contacts with them. However, in the event of an unfortunate encounter, we hope the first aid procedures described here will reduce the unpleasantness until professional help can be obtained.

How To Use This Guide

This guide can be used in two ways: first, as a resource for identifying general groups and specific species of venomous and toxic marine animals and second, as a first aid manual.

Identifying marine animals that exhibit a wide variety of shapes and forms is confusing for many beginners; however, once you can identify the major groups or phyla, species identification becomes somewhat easier. An outline of the major phyla that contain venomous and toxic marine species is shown on page 2. The reader should review each phylum description to obtain general information on the characteristics of marine organisms in that phylum.

Following the discussion of each major phylum, this guide provides individual species profiles of commonly encountered venomous and toxic species. It lists both the common and scientific names of each species. Although each species has only one scientific name, many species have several common names that differ among geographic areas. Generally, each species profile includes a photograph. Information on the physical characteristics of the species is summarized under **Description.** The geographic distribution and environment the animal inhabits are described under **Range and Habitat.** Information on similar species in other geographic areas is provided in some profiles under **Related Species.** The species' hazard rating to humans and any specific information on unique aspects of an envenomation, including symptoms and the individuals most at risk (e.g., divers, swimmers, fishermen, or reef walkers) are summarized under **Hazard to Humans.** We developed a system for ranking a species' potential hazard to humans using four hazard categories ranging from SLIGHT, to MODERATE, to SEVERE, to LETHAL. While this ranking system is subjective, it is based on a review of the reported severity of envenomations and incidence of fatalities, and will provide the reader with some expectation of the potential severity of contact. Lastly, specific means for avoiding contact are discussed under **Prevention.** For some groups of animals, methods of preventing contacts are similar for all members of the particular group (e.g., Scyphozoa jellyfish). In these cases, methods of preventing contact are presented under the general discussion for the group and additional information is provided under the species profile if warranted.

Since even the most careful individual may accidentally come in contact with a venomous or toxic species, the last section of the book provides

◄ *The majority of marine envenomations occur in the shallow coastal waters that are most frequented by man. Photograph by Paul Goetz.*

step-by-step first aid procedures for each of the major groups of venomous and toxic marine animals. Even if an animal cannot be identified to the species level, the reader can take some general steps by knowing to which major phylum the offending animal belongs. The first aid section also includes a list of items for a basic first aid kit and a list of emergency telephone numbers of agencies that can provide information or assistance with marine envenomations. The guide can thus be taken on a boat, to the beach, or carried in a dive bag for easy access in an emergency.

Major Phyla Containing Venomous and Toxic Marine Animals

Phylum Porifera—sponges
Phylum Cnidaria
   class anthozoa—corals and sea anemones
   class hydrozoa—hydroids, fire corals, and man-of-war
   class scyphozoa—true jellyfish
   class cubozoa—box jellyfish
Phylum Annelida—segmented worms
   class polychaeta—marine worms
Phylum Mollusca
   class gastropoda—snails
   class cephalopoda—octopuses and squids
Phylum Echinodermata
   class asteroidea—sea stars
   class echinoidea—sea urchins
   class holothuroidea—sea cucumbers
Phylum Chordata
   class chondrichthyes—sharks and stingrays
      family dasyatidae—whiptail stingrays
      family urolophidae—round stingrays (stingarees)
      family myliobatidae—eagle and cownose rays
      family gymnuridae—butterfly rays
   class osteichthyes—bony fishes
      family scorpaenidae—scorpionfish
      family uranoscopidae—stargazers
      family plotosidae—eel-tailed catfish
      family ariidae—sea catfish
      family siganidae—rabbitfish
      family trachinidae—weeverfish
   class reptilia—reptiles
      family hydrophiidae—sea snakes
      family laticaudidae—sea kraits

Tide pools are exciting places to explore, but for safety—don't touch any unfamiliar species. Photograph by Paul Goetz.

The Nature of Marine Envenomations

Through evolution, animals developed a variety of methods for securing their food and fending off predators. A wide variety of marine species developed the ability to produce venom and evolved specialized structures for effectively delivering the venom into a prey or predator. These venomous animals possess a diverse arsenal of fangs, body spines, specialized stinging cells called *nematocysts,* harpoon-like teeth, and chitinous beaks to deliver their venomous stings or bites. Other species, however, developed the ability to produce chemicals that are toxic to man, but these species do not possess the specialized structures needed for delivering these toxic chemicals. These toxic marine animals release toxic chemical secretions upon physical contact with their body wall or specific body organs. The toxic animals described in this guide include species of sponges (Phylum Porifera) and sea cucumbers (Phylum Echinodermata).

Venoms can be used for offensive (killing prey) and defensive (deterring predators) purposes or in some cases for both purposes. When used for offensive purposes, the envenomating structures are typically located near the mouth. For example, in sea anemones and jellyfish, the tentacles are covered with numerous stinging cells to stun and capture prey. Cones snails have hollow harpoon-shaped teeth to fire at prey, and sea snakes have venom glands and hollow fangs to deliver virulent bites to the small fishes on which they prey. In some cases when threatened, animals such as sea snakes also may use the only means at their disposal, their fangs, to deter a predator. For the most part, however, stings and bites to humans from venomous animals using these offensive systems are purely unintentional. Jellyfish are typically weak swimmers that drift at the mercy of the currents and tides and will sting any animal they come in contact with in their search for food. In contrast, when used for defensive purposes, the envenomating structures are generally found associated with the body surface, fins or tail of the animal. For example, sea urchin spines, fire worm bristles, and stingray and other venomous fish spines serve only to protect the animal from predation.

Worldwide, an estimated 50,000 envenomations by marine animals occur each year. This number does not include incidents in which the victims experience only minor discomfort and do not seek medical attention.

The most important characteristic of marine venoms is their potential to induce severe localized pain in humans. One point that must be emphasized is that the reaction of any victim to an envenomation is determined by several factors including the nature of the venom (type and virulence), the amount of venom introduced into the body, the site of the envenomation on the body, and the sensitivity of the victim to the specific venom.

The venoms produced by marine animals are extremely variable in their physical and chemical structure and in their virulence to humans. Venoms are proteins that may be very simple or very complex molecules and may be associated with several enzymes. Enzymes are molecules that are present in all living things and control the speed of many biochemical reactions in the body. The introduction of foreign enzymes of a venom upsets a victim's ability to control biochemical reactions in his or her own body. When the enzymes affect the central nervous system or circulatory system, the medical consequences can be severe and even life threatening.

Small variations in the structure of the venom protein molecule induced by heat or acid or basic conditions can alter the virulence of the venom. For some venoms, the application of heat or vinegar (mildly acidic) or dilute ammonia (mildly basic) to the wound site is sufficient to change or denature the structure of the venom and reduce its toxicity.

For several groups of marine animals, antivenoms have been developed that are highly effective in neutralizing the toxic effects of the venom. Antivenoms have been developed for sea snake bites, stonefish stings, and for stings of the deadly box jellyfish, *Chironex fleckeri.* Unfortunately, there are many other marine animals that produce virulent venom for which no antivenom has yet been developed. These include several species of Indo-Pacific blue-ringed octopus, several species of Indo-Pacific cones, and all families of stingrays and other bony fishes (excluding stonefish). Survival of victims of blue-ringed octopus bites and cone shell stings is ensured only if respiratory support can be obtained promptly and can be maintained until the venom's effects subside.

The amount of venom entering the victim's body is another factor in determining the severity of the envenomation. For example, while the Portuguese man-of-war's stinging cells are each less than $\frac{1}{25}$ inch (1 mm) in size, the fishing tentacles of this species may contain 750,000–1,000,000 stinging cells. The severity of a man-of-war sting depends on the length of the tentacle that comes in contact with the skin and how many of the stinging cells are triggered to inject venom into the victim.

The site of the bite or sting is a third factor that determines the severity of the envenomation. Often the effects are minimal when the envenomation occurs on the relatively thick, calloused skin of the hands and feet. However, reactions may be more severe on skin of the arms, legs, and torso, and most severe on the most sensitive skin areas of the neck, face, and lips.

Last, but most important, the sensitivity of the victim to a particular venom ultimately determines the severity of the envenomation. Just as with reactions to bee stings, some individuals may experience only minor pain and swelling around the sting or bite site, while others may require immediate medical attention to avoid death. Two factors that appear to

Underwater shipwrecks, wharfs, and other man-made structures are often covered with a variety of marine animals that can sting an unsuspecting diver. Photograph by Paul Goetz.

influence sensitivity are the age and physical condition of the victim. Young children and the elderly are usually at highest risk from envenomations. In addition, some victims may be allergic or hypersensitive to the venom of a particular marine species that is relatively harmless to most other people.

Although many readers may never experience anything more than a slight reaction to some of the venomous or toxic species described in this book, other, more sensitive individuals may experience severe and in some cases life-threatening reactions even to species with only slight to moderate hazard ratings. **Never underestimate the effect of an envenomation by any marine animal and be prepared to seek immediate medical attention for the victim when it is required.** For more details on first aid refer to **First Aid for Marine Envenomations** beginning on page 126.

Prevention

Prevention of marine envenomations involves the ability to recognize an animal as being venomous, to understand how the animal can envenomate you, and to know how to avoid a painful contact with the animal. Here are a few prevention steps:

1. Be able to identify the groups of venomous marine life in your locale and familiarize yourself with species in areas you plan to visit. Consult your local library for books on marine life. Remember: most injuries are avoidable—if you know which species to avoid.
2. Consult local lifeguards, divers, and boat captains for information on venomous marine life in areas you are visiting. Be attentive during pre-dive environmental briefings.

Wetsuits and lycra body suits provide protection from the stings of many venomous species particularly in tropical waters. Photograph by Paul Goetz.

At low tide, reef walkers explore the shallow waters off Heron Island, Australia. Some wear heavy shoes for protection from coral cuts and use a walking stick to probe the bottom to avoid stingrays or stonefish buried in the sediment. Photograph by Paul Goetz.

3. Visit an aquarium because this is the safest way to see venomous marine animals as they might appear underwater. Aquarium staff can provide additional information on local venomous species.

4. Don't touch any unfamiliar marine species. Never intentionally mistreat or provoke an attack from any marine animal because all species will defend themselves when threatened. Remember: even a gentle human touch can kill or injure many delicate animals, including coral polyps, that inhabit a coral reef.

5. Wear a wetsuit, lycra body suit, and gloves while diving or snorkeling, particularly in the tropics. These will prevent many painful contacts. Beachcombers and waders should wear protective shoes or wetsuit boots. Reef walkers should carry a stick to probe the bottom in front of them to frighten stingrays or other concealed fishes. Fishermen should wear heavy gloves when unhooking a venomous fish. Boaters should also wear gloves to avoid contact with hydroids or jellyfish that may foul mooring lines.

Porifera
Sponges

There are approximately 10,000 sponge species distributed worldwide and all but 150 are marine species. Sponges exhibit a wide variety of shapes including low profile encrusting forms, small spherical masses, single or branching tube-shaped forms often 5 feet (1.5 m) tall, and massive barrel-shaped giants that can conceal a diver. Sponges are the most primitive phylum of multicellular animals and, because of their sedentary habit, early biologists erroneously classified them as plants.

A sponge's body is constructed like a sieve that operates in reverse. Minute pores on the external surface of the sponge called *ostia* or incurrent pores allow water and planktonic food particles to pass through the sponge and into the body cavity. Once inside the body cavity, specialized cells with flagella capture and digest the food particles before the water is directed out through the *osculum* or excurrent pore. In some species there is a single large osculum at the top of the sponge, while in other species there are several smaller oscula through which water is expelled to the outside.

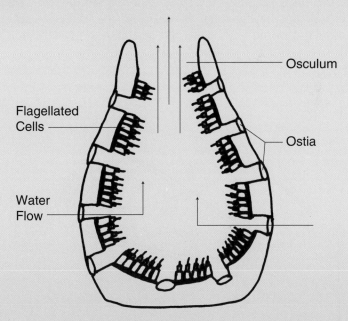

Sponge body in cross section.

As a group, sponges are generally easy to recognize. However, correct species identification is much more difficult because the shape of each sponge is influenced by the environmental factors to which it is exposed. These factors include the nature and inclination of the substrate to which the sponge is attached, the availability of space for growth, and the velocity and direction of water currents. In areas of strong currents, a species may form a small rounded or flattened mass, while in calm areas, individuals of the same species may assume a more vertical tree-like appearance. Thus, individuals of the same species often exhibit very different physical appearances under different environmental conditions.

Skeletal support for all sponges is provided by intermeshed spongin fibers made of protein, with additional support provided by siliceous or calcareous spicules. Because of their distinctive shapes, spicules are used in species classification. They may be needle-like rods with pointed, knobbed, or hooked ends or four- or six-rayed like children's jacks. Some biologists believe that skin abrasion by the sharp spicules contributes to the toxic reaction a sponge produces. Others contend the toxic reaction is produced only by contact with sponge secretions. This controversy remains unresolved. It may be that these two different mechanisms for toxicity operate either independently or jointly for different species of sponges.

Several toxic sponges are red to reddish-brown in color; however, as divers can attest, red is the first color to disappear visually underwater. At depths greater than 15 feet (4.5 m), red sponges appear brownish-gray. Thus, unless a diver is equipped with an underwater light, this striking red coloration will not be apparent. In addition, the exterior surface of a sponge may be covered with sand, silt, and marine growths that further conceal its color and appearance.

Sponge spicules

Hazard to Humans. Contact with toxic sponge secretions may produce skin rashes, swelling, redness, and itching. In severe cases, sensitive individuals may experience respiratory difficulties that require medical attention. Toxins in the slime secreted by some sponges also may be damaging to the eyes as well as causing contact dermatitis on areas of skin contact.

Prevention. Marine sponges should never be handled without gloves. This includes specimens handled underwater while they are alive, those that may have washed up on a beach after a storm, or those that have been dried. Toxicity of some species persists even after the animal has died and may reappear when the sponge is remoistened. Persons who are collecting sponges should never touch or sit on surfaces where sponges have been laying. Fishermen who trawl in areas where toxic sponges live and regularly collect them should wear safety glasses to prevent exposure of the eyes to slimy secretions. Long sleeve shirts, pants, and gloves should also be worn to ensure minimal skin contact.

First aid treatment for sponge contacts is given on page 126.

Do-Not-Touch-Me Sponge (*Neofibularia nolitangere*)

Description. The exterior surface of this sponge ranges in color from brick red to mahogany brown. The smooth outer surface has a lumpy appearance and the interior surface has a rough texture. These sponges are irregularly barrel-shaped and are often massive in size, reaching 36 inches (90 cm) in diameter and 15 inches (38 cm) or more in height. Characteristically, the sponge consists of one or more lobes with a single irregularly shaped opening at the top of each lobe. Small parasitic polychaete worms (*Haplosyllis* sp.) often inhabit the interior walls, and the yellow-line goby (*Gobiosoma horsti*) and shortstripe goby (*G. chancei*) often live in association with this sponge, feeding on these white worms.

Range and Habitat. This species inhabits coral reef areas in Florida, the Gulf of Mexico, and throughout the Caribbean from the low tide mark to a depth of 150 feet (46 m). Do-not-touch-me sponges commonly grow at the base of staghorn coral (*Acropora cervicornis*) and elkhorn coral (*A. palmata*).

Hazard to Humans. MODERATE TO SEVERE. Surface contact can produce an immediate stinging sensation. Numbness, swelling, severe burning, and blistering of the affected skin may last several days. In sensitive individuals, a severe itching reaction may be produced over the entire body.

11

Fire sponges are irregular in shape with individual lobes forming volcano-like projections. Photograph by Paul Humann.

◀ *Do-not-touch-me sponges are typically barrel-shaped with a single large osculum at the top of each lobe. Photograph by Nancy Sefton.*

Fire Sponge (*Tedania ignis*)

Description. The most striking characteristic of a fire sponge is its bright red-orange or reddish-brown color. The smooth outer surface of this sponge, which contains a few large pores, is soft and easily torn. Individual colonies are amorphous in structure, having no distinct shape and may be 4 to 12 inches (10 to 30 cm) in height and 12 inches (30 cm) wide.

Range and Habitat. Fire sponges are found in Florida, the Gulf of Mexico, and throughout the Caribbean area. This species is abundant in shallow bays and lagoons from the low tide mark to a depth of 50 feet (15 m). Fire sponges are often encountered in coral rubble areas adjacent to shallow patch reefs, in sea grass meadows, on rocks, on wharf pilings, and may also encrust mangrove roots.

Hazard to Humans. SLIGHT TO MODERATE. Surface contact may cause an immediate or delayed stinging sensation that can result in a painful rash. The rash, similar to poison ivy, can last for several days. In sensitive individuals, severe dermatitis may develop over the entire body.

Red moss sponges are very hardy and can withstand pollution and low salinities common in coastal bays and estuaries. Photograph by Andrew Martinez.

Red Moss Sponge (*Microciona prolifera*)

Description. This temperate water sponge is red to orange in color and grows by producing distinctive finger-like branches with fan-like or forked tips. Colonies first form as a thin layer encrusting hard substrates (e.g., rocks, wharf pilings, or oyster shells). As they increase in size, they form clusters up to 8 inches (20 cm) high and 10 inches (25 cm) in diameter with many fan-shaped branches. The small oscula are inconspicuous and are scattered over the surface of the sponge. In some areas, this species is also called the red beard sponge.

Range and Habitat. This widely distributed species occurs from Nova Scotia south along the Atlantic Coast to Florida and into the Gulf of Mexico as far west as Texas. It also occurs on the Pacific Coast from Washington south to central California. Red moss sponges are found in bays and estuaries on rock pilings or in association with oyster beds from the low tide mark to a depth of 90 feet (27 m).

Hazard to Humans. MODERATE. Repeated contact with this sponge may cause chronic dermatitis characterized by redness and stiffness of the skin and swelling in the finger joints. Fishermen and oystermen of the northeast Atlantic states commonly encounter this sponge while sorting their catch.

Cnidaria
Corals, Sea Anemones, Hydroids, Fire Corals, Man-of-War, Jellyfish, and Box Jellyfish

The phylum Cnidaria consists of 10,000 individual species and includes such highly diversified groups as the hard and soft corals, sea anemones, stinging hydroids, jellyfish, and box jellyfish. All members of this group have an internal digestive cavity, possess tentacles for feeding, and are radially symmetric. Two different body forms are exhibited: a sedentary polyp form like that found in corals, hydroids, and anemones and a free-swimming medusa stage like that of most jellyfish. Some members of this phylum exhibit both body forms during their life cycle, while other groups, through evolution, have eliminated one body form entirely. This phylum contains the largest number of venomous marine organisms. Some species have venom so virulent as to cause human deaths in a matter of several minutes. Repeated envenomations may result in increased sensitivity that can produce an anaphylactic reaction in some victims.

All Cnidaria possess stinging cells called *nematocysts* that range in length from $\frac{2}{1000}$ to $\frac{44}{1000}$ of an inch (0.05 to 1.12 mm). These specialized stinging cells are encapsulated in spheroid shaped cells (cnidocytes) that are most abundant on the tentacles and mouth parts. Some jellyfish species also possess nematocysts on the upper surface of the bell and some sea anemones have clusters of nematocysts on their body columns. The interior of the cnidocyte consists of a capsule containing an everted coiled tube with a short trigger bristle located at one end. The triggering mechanism that allows the stinging cell to discharge is activated by a combination of mechanical and chemical stimuli. Nematocysts are discharged from the capsule and may be used for anchoring, for defense, or for capturing prey. Over 30 distinct types of nematocysts have been identified. The most potent type is called a penetrant nematocyst and consists of a hollow venom tube. When the nematocyst is fired, the hollow tube penetrates the prey or victim's skin and injects a highly toxic venom.

The Cnidaria are divided into four major classes: **Anthozoa** (sea anemones, hard and soft coral), **Hydrozoa** (stinging hydroids, fire coral, and the Portuguese man-of-war), **Scyphozoa** (true jellyfish), and **Cubozoa** (box jellyfish). Each class contains a wide variety of species with distinct shapes, habits and great variations in the virulence of their venom. For these reasons, the suggested first aid treatments are also highly variable and are given separately for each class.

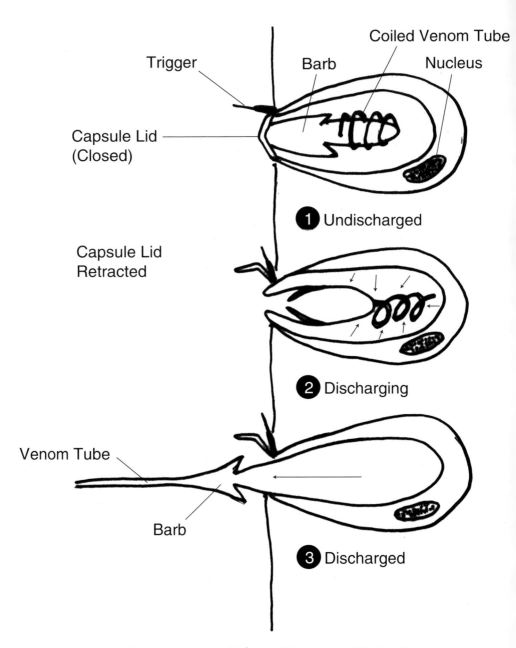

Trigger

Barb

Coiled Venom Tube

Nucleus

Capsule Lid
(Closed)

1 Undischarged

Capsule Lid
Retracted

2 Discharging

Venom Tube

Barb

3 Discharged

Structure of a Cnidarian nematocyst, (1) before, (2) during, and (3) after discharge.

Anthozoa
Corals and Sea Anemones

The class Anthozoa is an exclusively marine group that contains a wide variety of both solitary and colonial species. In members of this class, the sedentary polyp stage predominates and the free-swimming medusal stage is absent. The Anthozoa class contains over 65 percent of all Cnidarian species (more than 6,500 species) and includes such diverse animals as hard coral, soft corals (gorgonia), and sea anemones. Anthozoa species occur in all oceans, particularly in shallow coastal waters, and are widely distributed from warm tropic seas to cold polar waters. Within this class, only species of hard corals and sea anemones are venomous to man.

Hard Coral polyps are generally small and can be solitary or grow in extensive colonies containing thousands of individuals. Most coral species inhabit warm tropical or subtropical seas and are responsible for constructing the primary superstructure of fringing reefs, coral atolls, and barrier reefs such as the Great Barrier Reef of Australia. Hard corals are unique in their ability to secrete a calcium carbonate skeleton into which the live polyp may retract for protection. The hard skeletons come in a vast array of shapes and sizes and the resulting structure of the colony may be used in species identification.

Hazard to Humans. Like other Cnidarians, hard coral polyps contain nematocysts, but most are harmless to humans. However, the nematocysts may become much more of a hazard if the skin is cut deeply by the sharp coral skeleton and the nematocysts are introduced into the wound. Many species of coral in the genus *Acropora* have extremely sharp tips, particularly in areas of new growth, that can produce deep coral cuts in divers or snorkelers who carelessly come in contact with them.

Prevention. Wetsuits, lycra body suits, and gloves provide adequate protection from skin abrasions. Additional information is presented as appropriate in individual species profiles.

First aid treatment for coral cuts is given on page 126.

Sea Anemones are by far the more venomous members of the class Anthozoa. Sea anemones are typically large solitary polyps ranging from several inches to several feet across with colorful, flower-like bodies that attach to hard surfaces of a reef or to rocks. Unlike the hard corals, anemones lack the ability to secrete hard protective skeletons. The muscular cylindrical body column is attached to the substrate at one end by a basal disc. At the other end is the oral disc containing a central mouth surrounded by many tentacles. It is on these tentacles that the majority of nematocysts are located. Physical characteristics of the tentacles such as their size, shape, color, and number vary greatly among species and can be used in species identification.

Hazard to Humans. Surface contact with the tentacles of some anemone species can produce itching, redness of the skin and, in severe cases, blistering of the skin. Sea anemone nematocysts are highly variable with respect to their virulence and therefore the hazard to humans is also highly variable. The reader should review the discussion of Hazard to Humans in the individual species profiles.

Prevention. Wetsuits, lycra body suits, and gloves provide adequate protection from sea anemone stings. Additional information is presented as appropriate in individual species profiles.

First aid treatment for sea anemone stings is described on page 127.

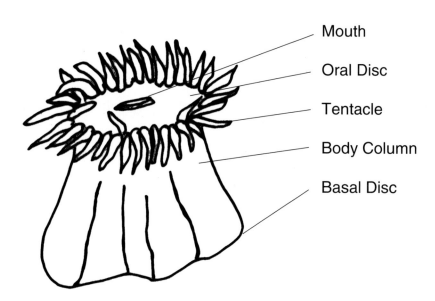

Mouth

Oral Disc

Tentacle

Body Column

Basal Disc

Structure of a sea anemone.

Elkhorn Coral (*Acropora palmata*)

Description. Colonies of this hard coral are tree-like in structure, some-times rising up to 10 feet (3 m) in vertical profile and branching more than 13 feet (4 m) horizontally. Although highly variable in shape, the colonies closely resemble the broad rack of antlers of an elk. The older coral polyps in a colony are mustard yellow to brown in color, with the youngest polyps on the rapidly growing branch tips being distinctively white due to the absence of zooanthellae (symbiotic algae growing within the coral's tissue). As the young polyps grow, they become the host organisms for zooanthellae, and the pigment from these symbiotic algae gives the coral polyps their color. Polyps of this coral are typically extended only at night. Under optimal conditions, this species grows rapidly at a rate of up to 6 inches (15 cm) a year.

Range and Habitat. Elkhorn coral are a major reef building compo-nent of Caribbean reef systems and are a common species in the Florida Keys, Bahamas, West Indies, and south to Brazil. This species proliferates in shallow water less than 40 feet (12 m) deep on windward coasts that receive constant wave or current action. If toppled by storm surge, broken fragments can regenerate to form new colonies. In some areas, the upper branches of the colonies may be exposed at low tide. Elkhorn coral may occur in small patches or cover many acres of reef.

Large colonies of elkhorn coral provide shelter for many coral reef fishes. Photograph by Anne DuPont.

The tentacles of individual staghorn coral polyps are visible in this close-up of a branch tip. Photograph by Pat Cunningham.

Hazard to Humans. SLIGHT TO MODERATE. Abrasions and deep cuts may result from contact with the tips of this species. It is these sharp tips that pose the greatest risk to snorkelers and divers who may inadvertently brush past a colony while swimming or may be thrown against a colony by wave action. Initial symptoms include a stinging sensation, redness, swelling, and itching of the wound site. Cuts and skin abrasions may be slow to heal and frequently become infected if not cleaned properly.

Prevention. Wetsuits, lycra body suits, and gloves provide adequate protection from skin abrasions. However, divers and snorkelers should avoid contact with this species not only to spare themselves pain and possible infection, but to protect the beauty of these fragile coral colonies. Divers should maintain good buoyancy control at all times. Diving or snorkeling should be avoided on shallow areas of these reefs at low tide or during periods when surge is excessive.

Staghorn Coral (*Acropora cervicornis*)

Description. Colonies of this hard coral closely resemble the pointed antlers of a deer or stag—from which the common name is derived. Loosely branched colonies may be 7 to 10 feet (2 to 3 m) high and spread 5 feet (1.5 m) wide. Colonies are composed of 1-inch (2.5 cm) diameter cylindrical branches usually yellow or brownish in color with white or lighter colored tips. These new areas of growth are white because they have not had time to acquire their resident symbiotic algae, the zooanthellae. The surface of this coral is covered by protruding calcareous cups that orient toward the sharp branch tips. Staghorn coral forms dense thickets of intermeshed branches that provide refuge for many small reef fish and invertebrates. This species also grows rapidly, up to 6 inches (15 cm) per year under optimal conditions. Polyps of this coral are extended only at night.

Range and Habitat. This common species is an important constituent of the shallow coral reef systems of the Florida Keys, the Bahamas, and the West Indies. Staghorn coral proliferates in protected windward areas and generally is found in calm water from 10 to 75 feet (3 to 23 m) deep. This extremely fragile coral is easily damaged, especially in areas heavily used by divers and snorkelers. Stands of staghorn coral may be exten-

Contact with the sharp tips of staghorn coral can result in deep coral cuts for divers. Good buoyancy control should be maintained for the protection of the diver and this delicate coral species. Photograph by Paul Goetz.

Despite its large size, the giant sea anemone of the tropical Atlantic is a relatively mild stinger. Photograph by Nancy Sefton.

sive and cover several acres or may occur in small isolated patches within a coral reef system.

Related Species. A total of 368 species of *Acropora* corals have been identified worldwide with 76 species reported from Australian waters alone. Two of these Indo-Pacific species are structurally almost identical to *A. cervicornis*. *A. nobilis* is staghorn-like with colonies being cream, brown, blue, yellow, or green in color. Each colony is a uniform color with pale branch tips. This species is very common in coral reef lagoons and on upper reef slopes. Large stands of this coral commonly cover many acres of reef. *A. nobilis* is found in tropical waters on both coasts of Australia, in the Coral Sea, and in the Western Pacific. *A. formosa* is another very common staghorn-like coral that forms dense thickets. It is often the dominant species found in lagoons and fringing reefs. This species occurs widely in the Indo-Pacific from the east coast of Africa throughout the Indian Ocean to Australia, the Coral Sea, and east to the Marshall Islands.

Hazard to Humans. SLIGHT TO MODERATE. (See Hazard to Humans for elkhorn coral on page 20.)

Prevention. Wetsuits, lycra body suits, and gloves provide adequate protection from skin abrasions. (See Prevention for elkhorn coral on page 20.)

Giant Sea Anemone (*Condylactis gigantea*)

Description. Largest of the sea anemones of the tropical Atlantic Ocean, the giant sea anemone can reach a diameter of 1 foot (30 cm). The tentacles may be 6 inches (15 cm) or longer and may be tipped with pink, blue, purple, or green. Coloration of the body column may vary from a pale blue-white to orange or bright red, although the column is often hidden within a protected reef crevice.

Range and Habitat. This species ranges from Bermuda south to Florida, the Bahamas and throughout the Caribbean. The giant sea anemone commonly occurs in mangrove areas, on coral reefs or in rocky shallow areas associated with eel or turtle grass meadows from 15 to 100 feet (5 to 30 m) deep. Various fish and shrimp species are found in association with this anemone, including the diamond blenny (*Malacoctenus boehlkei*), Pederson's cleaner shrimp (*Periclimenes pedersoni*), spotted cleaner shrimp (*P. yucatanicus*), red snapping shrimp (*Alpheus armatus*), and anemone shrimp (*Thor amboinensis*).

Hazard to Humans. SLIGHT. Reported to be a mild stinger; the sensitivity of the victim and site of the envenomation have a major influence on the reaction reported. Divers and snorkelers are most likely to encounter this species.

Pederson's cleaner shrimp are often found living among the tentacles of the giant sea anemone. Photograph by Paul Goetz.

Sun Anemone (*Stichodactyla helianthus*)

Description. This species is a flat, carpet-like anemone that is easily identified in the Caribbean. Except for a small area surrounding the central, oval-shaped mouth, the entire oral surface is covered by hundreds of tiny, round-tipped tentacles ½ inch (1.3 cm) long. The oral surface can attain a diameter of 10 inches (25 cm), but 6 inches (15 cm) is more typical. Coloration of the tentacles is highly variable ranging from light beige to pink, blue, or green.

Range and Habitat. Sun anemones occur throughout the Bahamas and the eastern and southern Caribbean region. This species thrives in shallow back reef areas at depths of 2 to 6 feet (0.6 to 1.8 m), although individuals have been collected as deep as 30 feet (9 m). Large aggregations of this anemone may be closely packed together in some reef areas. The anemone shrimp (*Thor amboinensis*) and banded clinging crab (*Mithrax cinctimanus*) are found in association with this anemone.

Hazard to Humans. SLIGHT TO MODERATE. This species feels sticky when touched with a calloused hand or finger; however, if tender skin of the torso or inside of the arms or legs is exposed to the nematocysts, a sharp stinging sensation is felt. Pain may persist for some time depending on the victim's sensitivity. The contact area may blister in severe cases. Divers, snorkelers, and swimmers may encounter this species.

The short, stubby tentacles of the carpet-like sun anemone are capable of producing blisters on sensitive skin. Photograph by Paul Humann.

Although the forked pseudotentacles of the branching anemone contain clusters of nematocysts, it is the primary unbranched tentacles extended at night that produce the more virulent stings. Photograph by Pat Cunningham.

Branching Anemone (*Lebrunia danae*)

Description. This anemone, though not an uncommon tropical Atlantic species, is seldom seen because of its habit of dwelling in reef crevices. Branching anemones attain a maximum diameter of 12 inches (30 cm). Unlike most other anemones, they possess two distinct types of tentacles: long, unbranched, primary tentacles typical of most anemones, and branched pseudotentacles with forked tips that contain nematocyst-filled nodules. During the day, the pseudotentacles, which contain zooanthellae, are extended to obtain sunlight for photosynthesis. In contrast, the primary tentacles are extended at night to capture zooplankton. It is these primary tentacles that produce a potent sting.

Range and Habitat. Branching anemones range from Bermuda south to the Bahamas, throughout the Caribbean, and south to Brazil. They are commonly found in water 6 to 130 feet (2 to 40 m) deep and are always found camouflaged in a reef crevice with just the pseudotentacles exposed.

Hazard to Humans. MODERATE TO SEVERE. This species is one of the most venomous of the Atlantic anemones. Contact produces localized burning and itching of the skin followed by redness and swelling. In severe envenomations, fever, chills, abdominal pain, nausea, vomiting, headaches, and prostration can occur. Divers may be stung inadvertently while reaching into crevices.

Ringed Anemone (*Bartholomea annulata*)

Description. Although the short body column is generally hidden from view in a reef crevice, the numerous (up to 200) long, thin tentacles are usually visible. An individual with its tentacles spread may reach a diameter of 8 inches (20 cm). The slender transparent tentacles are up to 4 inches (10 cm) long and are covered with discontinuous bands of whitish nematocysts. These incomplete rings of nematocysts visually appear to be wrapped around each tentacle in a corkscrew-like arrangement. For this reason, this species is also commonly called the corkscrew anemone. Tissues of this anemone are a transparent light brown, which is in part due to the presence of zooanthellae.

Range and Habitat. The ringed anemone may be the single most common anemone in the tropical Atlantic region and ranges from Bermuda, south to the Bahamas, into the Caribbean, Gulf of Mexico, and south to Brazil. This species is found in reef crevices, in sand channels, or on isolated coral heads in sea grass meadows from a depth of 3 to 120 feet (1 to 37 m). Red snapping shrimp (*Alpheus armatus*) and Pederson's cleaner shrimp (*Periclimenes pedersoni*) are found associated with this anemone.

Hazard to Humans. SLIGHT TO MODERATE. Reports vary as to the severity of a sting, although it is generally considered to be mild. Divers and snorkelers are most likely to encounter this species.

Turtle Grass Anemone (*Viatrix globulifera*)

Description. Both the tentacles and body column of this inconspicuous anemone are translucent to transparent white in color. The extremely small oral disc ranges in size from ¼ to ¾ inches (0.6 to 2 cm) across. As its name implies, it is commonly found anchored to blades of turtle grass or other underwater growth. The scientific name may be synonymous with *Bundodeopsis antilliensis*.

Range and Habitat. This anemone is commonly found in quiet shallow bays in Florida, the Bahamas, and the Caribbean region from below the low tide mark to 20 feet (6 m) deep. It is very common in some areas of Florida Bay.

◀ *The ringed anemone is aptly named for the pattern of stinging nematocysts that almost completely encircles each tentacle. Photograph by Pat Cunningham.*

Turtlegrass anemones produce a potent sting, but because of their small size, their victims may never know what stung them. Photograph by Pat Cunningham.

Hazard to Humans. MODERATE TO SEVERE. This anemone's diminutive size allows it to go unnoticed by most victims until they have been stung. Even after being stung, it is often difficult to locate the offending organism. Multiple stings raised quarter-sized welts on the author's legs that persisted for almost six hours. Divers, snorkelers, swimmers, and waders in shallow bays are most likely to encounter this virulent stinger.

Feathery Sea Anemone (*Actinodendron plumosum*)

Description. The grayish-green body column of this large sand-dwelling anemone can attain 12 inches (30 cm) in height and 24 inches (60 cm) in width. When extended, the light brown to grayish-green multi-branched tentacles give the flower-like appearance of a soft coral. This anemone is able to retract its body column completely into the sand leaving a small hole 1½ inches (4 cm) in diameter. In a semi-retracted state, it takes on the appearance of a flattened top hat. In some areas, this virulent stinger is aptly called hell's fire anemone.

With its tentacles extended, the feathery sea anemone closely resembles a clump of soft coral. Photograph by Neville Coleman.

Range and Habitat. The feathery sea anemone is found in tropical waters of the Indo-Pacific region. Its preferred habitat includes sheltered places (e.g., under coral ledges) on intertidal or subtidal sand flats adjacent to coral reefs at depths up to 45 feet (14 m).

Hazard to Humans. SEVERE. The highly virulent sting produces extremely painful welts and skin ulcerations. Swelling and soreness of the affected skin can last for a week. In severe cases, ulcerations may take several months to heal completely. Reef walkers, snorkelers, and divers are at greatest risk.

Prevention. Wetsuits, lycra body suits, and gloves provide adequate protection for divers and snorkelers; reef walkers should wear sturdy shoes or wetsuit boots.

Hydrozoa
Hydroids, Fire Corals, and Man-of-War

The class Hydrozoa, which contains almost 30 percent of all Cnidarian species, encompasses the most diverse group of venomous species and includes the stinging hydroids, hydrocorals (fire corals), and the virulent siphonophore, the Portuguese man-of-war. Most members of this class (2,700 species) are inconspicuous in size and coloration, and the sedentary polyp phase of the life cycle predominates.

Stinging Hydroid polyps are extremely small and are borne on the stem and lateral branches of feather or fern-like colonies. The specific configuration of the polyps on the lateral branches and the arrangement of the lateral branches on the primary stem are used to classify different species. Unwary divers are often stung when brushing against these inconspicuous organisms that are found attached to wharves, pilings, rocks, shipwrecks, and permanently submerged mooring lines.

Hydrocorals include the fire corals that secrete calcareous skeletons similar to those of hard corals. The hydrocoral's skeleton, however, is covered with thousands of tiny pores from which the genus *Millepora* (thousand pores) derives its name. Two types of cells protrude from the minute pores: feeding polyps and offensive (stinging) polyps. Short, stout feeding polyps contain a mouth surrounded by several clusters of nematocysts. Each feeding polyp is encircled by 5 to 9 long, slender, offensive polyps covered with clusters of nematocysts. Fire coral contacts result in painful stings to a large number of divers and snorkelers annually.

Siphonophores are colonial hydrozoans that either swim in midwater or float at the surface buoyed up by a gas-filled float. The well-known Portuguese man-of-war, which resembles a jellyfish, is really a colonial organism composed of several different types of polyps. Tentacles, densely covered with nematocysts, hang from the float and can reach 60 to 90 feet (18 to 27 m) in length. Often by the time a victim sees the float, contact with the tentacles has already occurred. This species is by far the most virulent hydrozoan worldwide and human fatalities have occurred.

Hazard to Humans. The hazard to humans is highly variable for various hydrozoans. See the individual species profiles for specific hazard information.

Prevention. Wet suits, lycra body suits, and gloves provide adequate protection from most hydrozoan stings. Additional information on methods of preventing contacts will be provided as appropriate in individual species profiles.

First aid treatment for hydroid and fire coral stings is given on page 127 and first aid treatment for man-of-war stings is given on page 128.

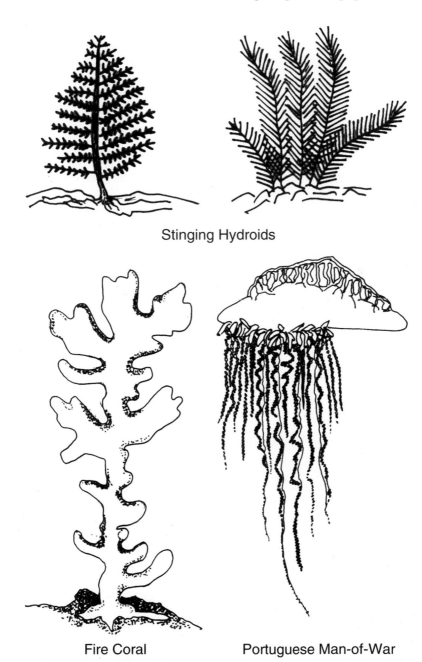

Stinging Hydroids

Fire Coral   Portuguese Man-of-War

Members of the class Hydrozoa.

Cypress Sea Fern (*Aglaophenia cupressina*)

Description. This species is one of the largest tropical hydroids with colonies growing in large clumps attached to a variety of hard substrates. The fern-like fronds ranging in color from a yellow green to green to a light brown are typically 6 to 12 inches (15 to 30 cm) long, however, some colonies can grow up to 3 feet (1 m) across. Underwater, this species looks like a large clump of seaweed. The common name is derived from the similarity in appearance of its branches to those of a cypress tree; however, the species is also commonly called stinging seaweed.

Range and Habitat. Widely distributed in both tropical and subtropical waters of the Indo-Pacific region, this hydroid is found in sheltered back reef areas and in lagoons, but can also occur on moderately deep reefs at depths of 85 feet (26 m). Cypress sea ferns range throughout the Indo-Pacific region including the entire length of the Great Barrier Reef from Heron Island to Cape York. They are extremely common at the Cod Hole, a popular dive site off Lizard Island.

Hazard to Humans. MODERATE TO SEVERE. The sting is immediately painful; however, victims must also endure a protracted period of itching that may persist for up to a month. Divers and snorkelers are at greatest risk from contact. After severe storms, fragments of this hydroid may break off and drift in the sea, posing a hazard to swimmers and waders.

When seen underwater, the cypress sea fern could easily be mistaken for a clump of green seaweed. Photograph by Paul Goetz.

White stinging sea fern colonies often grow in areas where surge and currents predominate. Photograph by Pat Cunningham.

White Stinging Sea Fern (*Lytocarpus phlllppinus*)

Description. This hydroid is easily recognized by the white bush-like colonies of delicate fronds that grow in clumps and can attain a height of 18 inches (45 cm). The primary stem and side branches are black or dark brown and are covered with tiny white polyps. The primary stem of each colony arises from a single horny base that is anchored to a hard substrate on the reef. This stinging hydroid is aptly known as fireweed in some areas.

Range and Habitat. This virulent stinger is found widely throughout the Indo-Pacific region. Its preferred habitat includes reef edges or areas along reef channels where surge and strong currents are prevalent. Colonies are found subtidally to a depth of 100 feet (30 m).

Related Species. A related species, Nutting's stinging hydroid (*Lytocarpus nuttingi*) is found in the eastern Pacific from Southern California south to the Gulf of California. The white, feather-like colonies attain a height of 12 inches (30 cm) and closely resemble *L. philippinus.*

Hazard to Humans. MODERATE TO SEVERE. The sting is immediately painful and produces a red rash, swelling, and blistering that persists for several days. Victims of severe envenomations must also endure a protracted period of itching that may persist for more than a month. Divers and snorkelers are at greatest risk from contact with this species and the hands, wrists, and ankles are the skin areas most commonly stung.

Branching Hydroid (*Sertularella speciosa*)

Description. Colonies of this large Atlantic hydrozoan can be 8 inches (20 cm) high and 6 inches (15 cm) wide. They may grow solitary or in small clumps. The yellow to tan colored, feather-like colonies are evenly branched and grow in a single plane. The primary stem has numerous side branches that grow alternately and almost at right angles to the primary stem. Polyps of this species are small in size, contain 12 slender basal tentacles, and grow alternately along the top and bottom of the side branches and primary stem.

Range and Habitat. Branching hydroids are found in Bermuda, Florida, and throughout the Caribbean region, particularly in areas of moderate current flow. This hydroid prefers disturbed surfaces and encrusts rocks, coral heads, and other hard substrates at depths from 30 to 100 feet (9 to 30 m).

Hazard to Humans. SLIGHT. This species produces a mildly toxic stinging sensation when touched. Affected skin areas may become red and inflamed, but in severe envenomations, blistering may result in sensitive individuals. Divers and snorkelers are most at risk around wrecks, wharfs, and other underwater structures where this species thrives.

Christmas Tree Hydroid (*Halocordyle disticha*)

Description. This aptly named hydroid forms Christmas-tree-shaped colonies up to 5 inches (13 cm) in height with a terminal polyp on the brown primary stalk just like the angel atop a Christmas tree. Colonies exhibit alternate pinnate branching in one plane and usually grow in small clusters. Fine hair-like tentacles can be seen upon close inspection of the spherical-shaped white polyps. The polyps are naked, lacking a protective skeletal capsule.

Range and Habitat. The Christmas tree hydroid is a tropical species that ranges from Florida south to Brazil. In reef areas with moderate current flow, this hydroid is very common at depths ranging from 10 to 60 feet (3 to 18 m). Colonies are found on disturbed surfaces including dead coral heads, shipwrecks, or other underwater man-made structures. Bushy colonies are also observed under reef ledges, at cave entrances, or on vertical reef surfaces.

◄ *Branching hydroids prefer growing on disturbed surfaces in areas of moderate current flow. Photograph by Pat Cunningham.*

Christmas tree hydroids are common on disturbed surfaces such as shipwrecks or on dead coral or gorgonia colonies. Photograph by Pat Cunningham.

Hazard to Humans. SLIGHT. A mild stinging sensation is produced on the skin. Affected areas may become red and inflamed temporarily, and blistering may occur in sensitive individuals. Divers are most likely to encounter this species.

Solitary Gorgonian Hydroid (*Ralpharia gorgoniae*)

Description. This hydroid is characterized by a large single pinkish-white polyp with about two dozen slender, translucent tentacles radiating from its center. The tips of these long tentacles are often curled slightly. Upon contact, all the tentacles are curled up toward the polyp's center. Solitary polyps of this species are ½ to 1 inch (1.3 to 2.5 cm) in diameter and grow only at the tips of soft coral branches such as sea plumes (*Pseudopterogorgia* sp.). Although several of these hydroids may grow on the same soft coral colony, no more than one individual polyp will grow on each branch tip.

The beautiful and delicate solitary gorgonian hydroid has the reputation of being one of the most potent stingers among the Atlantic hydroids. Photograph by Nancy Sefton. ▶

Range and Habitat. This stinging hydroid is found throughout the Caribbean at depths ranging from 15 to 65 feet (5 to 20 m). It is primarily confined to reef areas where soft corals (gorgonia) grow in abundance.

Hazard to Humans. MODERATE TO SEVERE. This diminutive hydroid produces a highly potent sting to bare skin. Divers are most likely to encounter this species.

Fire Coral (*Millepora complanata, M. alcicornis, and M. squarrosa*)

Description. These three tropical hydrocorals closely resemble hard corals, but are actually members of the class Hydrozoa. Fire corals have light brownish to creamy yellow colonies highlighted by distinctive white tips. The exterior surface appears smooth with hair-like tentacles projecting through the hard calcareous skeleton. Atlantic fire corals have been classified into three separate species because three distinct growth forms occur; however, some taxonomists believe that the branching fire coral, *M. alcicornis* and the box fire coral, *M. squarrosa* may be ecological variants of blade fire coral, *M. complanata* rather than distinct species. *M. complanata* grows in blade or plate-like vertical branches from 1 to 18 inches (3 to 46 cm) in height that are connected only at their bases. *M. alcicornis* is a branching form that often grows finger-like in a single plane or branched in several planes and also encrusts the surface of glass bottles, shells, sea fans, or other coral heads, assuming the shape of the encrusted animal or object. And the third and rarest form, *M. squarrosa* produces colonies with multiple, box-like partitions or encrusts a substrate with a wrinkled, purplish-tan veneer ¾ to 1¼ inches (2 to 3 cm) thick.

Range and Habitat. Fire corals are dominant members of shallow coral reef communities. Branching and blade fire coral are most commonly encountered in Florida, the Bahamas, and the Caribbean region. Blade fire coral, in particular, prefers shallow reef areas from 3 to 45 feet (1 to 14 m) where wave action and surge are high, and are nearly awash at low tide. Branching fire coral is generally found in moderately deep water, more than 30 feet (9 m), and is less often encountered in areas of high surge. Box fire coral inhabits reef tops particularly in areas with water movement or regular surge and occurs from the Dominican Republic south to Brazil.

Related Species. Several related fire corals occur in habitats similar to those occupied by their Caribbean cousins. These species are widely dis-

The hair-like stinging tentacles of the branching fire coral are clearly seen protruding through pores in the smooth calcareous skeleton. Photograph by Pat Cunningham. ▶

The white tips and smooth surface texture of blade fire coral easily distinguishes it from true hard corals. Photograph by Paul Goetz.

tributed in shallow tropical waters of the Indo-Pacific region. *Millepora platyphylla* is a massive, blade or plate-like fire coral similar in appearance to *M. complanata. M. dichotoma* and *M. tenera* are branching forms closely resembling *M. alcicornis.*

Hazard to Humans. MODERATE TO SEVERE. Contact with a live fire coral colony may cause a severe burning sensation. Skin may remain tender and inflamed for several days and blistering may occur in sensitive individuals. Fire coral stings are most severe on the sensitive body areas (i.e., inside of the arms and legs, torso, neck, and face) while envenomations to the calloused palms of the hands and soles of the feet may not even be felt. The Divers Alert Network (DAN) reported that a diver suffered a severe allergic reaction after contact with fire coral. After ascending, the diver began coughing up blood and experienced acute chest pain.

Prevention. Divers, snorkelers, and swimmers should be particularly careful when diving in areas where surge may carry them into contact with these species. Wetsuits, lycra body suits, and gloves provide adequate protection.

Portuguese Man-of-War (*Physalia physalis*)

Description. The Portuguese man-of-war, although superficially resembling a jellyfish, is actually a member of the class Hydrozoa. The man-of-war appears to be a single animal, but is actually a colonial organism composed of three distinct types of semi-independent polyps. Each type of polyp is specialized to perform a specific function: reproduction, digestion, or capturing prey. These three types of polyps are attached to the base of an elongated gas-filled bluish float. The float can be 12 inches (30 cm) high and 6 inches (15 cm) wide and buoys up the entire colony. In large individuals, each fishing tentacle (offensive polyp) can be 60 to 90 feet (18 to 27 m) long and may contain as many as 750,000 to 1,000,000 nematocysts, which are used to sting prey. After the fishing tentacles have captured a fish, the prey is drawn upward toward the float where the feeding polyps surround it completely with their transparent membranous lips. Once enveloped by the feeding polyps, digestive enzymes are secreted onto the prey, disintegrating its tissues so that it can be absorbed by the feeding polyps and distributed to all members of the colony. Despite the virulent sting, the man-of-war fish, *Nomeus gronovi,* often finds refuge from its own predators among the tentacles. Two other species, the blue glaucus nudibranch, *Glaucus marinus,* and the small purple sea snail, *Janthina janthina,* consume the virulent nematocysts while foraging on the tentacles without showing any ill effects.

Range and Habitat. The man-of-war is a circumtropical species. It is common in the tropical Atlantic Ocean and is very common in the Florida Keys and throughout the central Florida region. Large flotillas of this hydrozoan are transported by warm tropical currents to temperate coasts where they are washed ashore by storms or onshore winds. Along the east coast of Florida, large numbers of the man-of-war are blown ashore during the late winter and early spring months (February, March, and April) with east winds. Occasionally, they are carried by the Gulf Stream current as far north as the Bay of Fundy in Canada. This species is also found in the tropical Indo-Pacific region. The pelagic man-of-war drifts at the surface of the sea, fishing for its prey of small fish. Having no ability to propel itself through the water, it is at the mercy of the winds, tides, and currents.

Related Species. Some taxonomists have identified a smaller Indo-Pacific species as *Physalia utricula;* others believe there is only one circumtropical species.

Hazard to Humans. SEVERE TO LETHAL. This is the most virulent hydrozoan species found worldwide. Whether encountered in the water or washed up on a beach, the nematocysts can be discharged by physical

contact thereby injecting venom into the victim. Divers, snorkelers, swimmers, fishermen, and beachcombers are all at risk in areas where this species occurs. Young children and the elderly are likely to be most sensitive to the venom. Stings are extremely painful and may cause welts, swelling, and blistering of the skin. Some victims describe the contact as feeling like a red hot piece of wire is touching the skin. Various symptoms have been reported including chills and fever, headache, and shock. In severe cases, respiratory distress, muscle cramps, paralysis, and death from cardiac arrest have occurred. Victims should be removed from the water immediately to prevent drowning and medical attention should be obtained promptly.

Prevention. Divers, snorkelers, and swimmers must be especially careful in waters where the man-of-war floats are observed at the surface because the fishing tentacles can extend almost 100 feet (30 m) from the surface float. Divers should be careful when surfacing to avoid being entangled in the long tentacles. Boaters and fishermen should be careful when retrieving anchor lines and fishing gear. Beachcombers also must be alert to the man-of-war washed ashore after storms because the nematocysts remain active long after the animal has died. Wetsuits, lycra body suits, and gloves provide the best protection from contact.

◄ *The man-of-war is a highly venomous stinger that can inflict painful stings even several weeks after the colony has been washed ashore and the tentacles have dried out on the sand. Photograph by Paul Goetz.*

The transparent bluish float of a man-of-war partially conceals the deadly fishing tentacles that can trail more than 90 feet below it. Photograph by Paul Goetz.

Scyphozoa
True Jellyfish

The Scyphozoa or true jellyfish are solitary organisms. As adults they assume the medusal or free-swimming phase, while during their brief larval stage, they live in a sedentary polyp form. The medusal stage of this exclusively marine class is the dominant and conspicuous stage in the life cycle. The majority of scyphozoans inhabit coastal waters and many become an annoyance to man when they invade bathing beaches during the summer months. There are about 250 species of jellyfish inhabiting the coastal waters of the world from cold polar waters throughout the temperature zone to warm tropical seas.

These jellyfish have transparent bells that may be flattened and plate-like or bowl-shaped in appearance. Tentacles, heavily armed with stinging nematocysts, hang from the margin of the bell and their shape, length, arrangement, and number vary greatly among species. In the center of the underside of each bell is the square-shaped mouth located at the end of the feeding tube. The corners of the mouth can be folded into four frilly oral arms. Like the tentacles, the oral arms contain nematocysts to stun and entangle prey, which is then enveloped in mucus, conveyed to the mouth and into the gastric cavity where digestion occurs.

Most jellyfish are moderately weak swimmers that move at the mercy of the wind, waves, and tides in open waters. They propel themselves through the water by rhythmic contractions of the bell. Because many species are light sensitive, they use these contractions of the bell to vary their depth during the day. Members of this group include some of the most venomous organisms in the sea.

Hazard to Humans. Reactions differ greatly depending on the species encountered and the sensitivity of the victim. Pain, burning, and blistering of the skin, chills and fever, and headaches are typical symptoms of a contact. In severe cases, shock, respiratory distress, paralysis, and cardiac arrest may result. As a precaution, victims should be removed from the water immediately to prevent drowning.

Prevention. Wetsuits, lycra body suits, and gloves provide adequate protection from most scyphozoan stings. First aid treatment for jellyfish stings is given on pages 128–129.

By any standard of size or virulence of the venom, the lion's mane jellyfish is an impressive marine animal and one that should command respect. Photograph by Herb Segars. ▶

Lion's Mane Jellyfish (*Cyanea capillata*)

Description. This is the largest jellyfish in the world. Individuals 8 feet (2.4 m) in diameter have been reported. The saucer-shaped bell is typically 3 feet (1 m) in diameter and 2 feet (60 cm) high and the margin of the bell is divided into eight lobes. Arranged in eight U-shaped clusters along the bell margin, the more than 160 slender tentacles may be up to 90 feet (27 m) long. The bell color varies with age of the medusa: pink to yellow in juveniles up to 5 inches (13 cm), reddish to yellow-brown in individuals up to 18 inches (46 cm), and dark red-brown to purple in adults over 18 inches (46 cm) in diameter. Copious mucus secreted by the oral arms has a strong fishy odor.

Range and Habitat. A cosmopolitan species, this jellyfish is found in temperate waters of both the Atlantic and Pacific Oceans. Lion's mane jellyfish float near the surface and large wind-drifted swarms can appear periodically in coastal areas. High concentrations of young medusa appear annually during June and July in the northern hemisphere.

Hazard to Humans. SEVERE TO LETHAL. Stings are highly toxic and contact results in localized pain, blistering and burning of the skin. Severe envenomations may cause headaches, severe muscle cramps, shock, respiratory distress, paralysis, and cardiac arrest. Victims should be removed from the water immediately to prevent drowning. Divers, snorkelers, and swimmers are at greatest risk. When remoistened, tentacle fragments dried on fishing nets can sting on contact and are a hazard to fishermen.

The translucent moon jelly can grow to the size of a large dinner plate, and large swarms are common in bays and estuaries during certain times of the year. Photograph by Paul Humann.

Moon Jelly (*Aurelia aurita*)

Description. The flat, saucer-shaped, translucent bell of the moon jelly may reach a diameter of 16 inches (40 cm). Numerous branching radial canals are clearly visible within the translucent flesh of the bell. In addition, four horseshoe-shaped reproductive organs at the center of the bell form a distinctive four-leaf clover pattern, which is the most striking feature of this species. Ripe female gonads are yellow-pink to violet, male gonads are yellow-brown to rose, while immature gonads are white. A single row of short, hair-like tentacles forms a fringe around the entire scalloped margin of the bell. The central mouth consists of a short feeding tube surrounded by four long frilly oral arms.

Range and Habitat. This pelagic species floats near the surface in Atlantic coastal areas from cold Arctic waters, south to Florida, and into the Gulf of Mexico and along the Pacific Coast from Alaska to southern California. Single individuals may be observed year-round, and large swarms may appear in bays and estuaries during summer months.

Hazard to Humans. SLIGHT. Skin contact causes a mild rash and itching that may persist for several hours. During the summer, dense swarms of moon jelly may clog fishing trawls. Divers, snorkelers, swimmers, and fishermen are most likely to encounter this species.

Mangrove Upside-Down Jellyfish (*Cassiopeia xamachana*)

Description. The bell of this jellyfish can attain a maximum diameter of 12 inches (30 cm) and varies in color from light green to dark brown. On the dorsal surface of the bell, alternating dark- and light-colored rays radiate from the center. This jellyfish, as its name suggests, has the unusual habit of lying upside down on the bottom of shallow lagoons and by doing so obtains sunlight for the symbiotic photosynthetic algae. These algae are contained within the hundreds of lacy extensions of the oral arms that radiate from the central mouth. The oral arms are one and one half times the bell's radius. This jellyfish lacks tentacles; however, potent clusters of nematocysts are concentrated along the margin of the bell.

Range and Habitat. Mangrove upside-down jellyfish are commonly found in Florida, the Gulf of Mexico, and the Caribbean. They are typically found in shallow, semi-stagnant waters of tropical bays or mangrove

Snorkelers often see large numbers of mangrove upside-down jellyfish covering the bottom of shallow lagoons in Florida Bay. Photograph by Paul Humann.

swamps from the low tide mark to a depth of 20 feet (6 m). In the upside-down position, this species closely resembles a sea anemone.

Related Species. Two species that closely resemble *C. xamachana* in appearance are the upside-down sea jelly, (*C. andromeda*) of the Indo-Pacific region and the upside-down jellyfish (*C. frondosa*) of Florida, the Bahamas, and the Caribbean region. The bell of the Indo-Pacific species can attain a diameter of 12 inches (30 cm), while that of the Caribbean species can attain a diameter of 10½ inches (26 cm). Both inhabit sandy or sandy-mud flats in shallow water areas to a depth of 25 feet (8 m).

Hazard to Humans. MODERATE TO SEVERE. Contact produces uncomfortable tingling sensations in the lips and skin. The onset of the tingling sensation occurs more rapidly with each succeeding exposure. In areas where this jellyfish occurs, densities of 10 to 30 individuals per square yard (12 to 35 individuals per m^2) are not uncommon. Swimmers, waders, snorkelers, and divers are most at risk.

Purple Jellyfish (*Pelagia noctiluca*)

Description. The hemispherical bell of this species ranges in color from a rosy pink to purple to yellow. Scattered clusters of nematocysts on the dorsal surface of the 4-inch (10 cm) bell give it a warty appearance. The margin of the bell has 16 lobes that alternately contain either one of the eight long pink tentacles or one of the eight marginal sense organs. The tentacles are sometimes more than 3 feet (1 m) long. The long, thick feeding tube extends below the bell as four frilly, pink oral arms surrounding the mouth. At night, this species is luminescent, and large swarms appear as glowing white balls at the surface of the sea. This species is also called the warty jellyfish.

Range and Habitat. Although the purple jellyfish is generally encountered at the surface of the open ocean, it is occasionally washed ashore by storms. This circumtropical species may be encountered in coastal waters of the Atlantic and Pacific oceans and the Mediterranean Sea.

Hazard to Humans. SLIGHT TO MODERATE. Stings from this species are mildly toxic. Divers, snorkelers, and swimmers generally do not encounter this offshore species unless it is washed into coastal bays by waves or currents. Purple jellyfish entangled in fishing gear and trawls are a hazard to fishermen.

A denizen of surface waters of the open ocean, the purple jellyfish is encountered only occasionally in coastal areas. Photograph by Paul Humann. ▶

Sea Nettle (*Chrysaora quinquecirrha*)

Description. The sea nettle's milky white bowl-shaped bell is 10 inches (25 cm) in diameter, 5 inches (13 cm) high, and has 40 long yellow tentacles. Sometimes pink markings are visible radiating outward from the center of the bell like spokes of a wheel. A smaller white bay form is 4 inches (10 cm) in diameter, 2 inches (5 cm) high, and has only 24 tentacles. This may be a juvenile stage. Unlike many jellyfish, the dorsal surface of the bell is covered with numerous clusters of potent nematocysts.

Range and Habitat. This species ranges from New England south to Florida, including Bermuda, through the Gulf of Mexico to Brazil. The occurrence of dense swarms of sea nettles regularly cause beach closures in the Chesapeake Bay during July and August.

Hazard to Humans. MODERATE TO SEVERE. When it occurs in swarms, this species is hazardous to swimmers and divers. While the venom is moderately toxic, producing mild skin irritation, a person stung repeatedly may require hospitalization. Severe envenomations may cause chills and fever, headache, shock, severe muscle cramps, respiratory distress, paralysis, and cardiac arrest. Victims should be removed from the water immediately to prevent drowning.

During the summer, dense swarms of sea nettles cause the closing of many swimming beaches in the Chesapeake Bay. Photograph by Miami Seaquarium.

Cubozoa
Box Jellyfish

Unlike the typical plate or bowl-shaped bells characteristic of most Scyphozoans, the Cubozoans, or box jellyfish, have a box-shaped bell. The margin of the bell is unfrilled. Each of the lower corners of the bell has a tough, gelatinous lobe or pedalium to which one or more tentacle filaments are attached. Although taxonomists originally placed the box jellyfish into the class Scyphozoa, distinct differences in their nematocysts and life cycle led to their reclassification into a separate class, Cubozoa.

Of all of the venomous cnidarian species described in this guide, only the man-of-war, lion's mane jellyfish, and sea nettle possess venom as virulent as that of some species of box jellyfish. Approximately 16 distinct species of box jellyfish exist worldwide. Although envenomations by one of the less virulent Atlantic species can be extremely dangerous and can result in hospitalization of the victim, envenomations by some of the related Indo-Pacific species can be fatal within 3 to 5 minutes unless antivenom injections are administered immediately. The potential hazard and distress that these box jellyfish can cause is compounded because they often occur in swarms. Reactions to envenomations by box jellyfish differ greatly depending on the species encountered, the sensitivity of the victim, the area of the body envenomated, and the number of stings to the victim. The most sensitive areas of the body include the neck and the face.

Hazard to Humans. Although reactions differ greatly among victims, excruciating pain, respiratory distress, cardiac arrest, coma, and death may result. Victims should be removed from the water immediately to prevent drowning, and medical attention should be sought promptly for severe envenomations. Divers engaged in a night dive or individuals swimming around a lighted dock after dark are most at risk. See additional information on hazards in the individual species profiles.

Prevention. Extreme care should be taken to avoid any contact with a box jellyfish species. Divers are protected by wetsuits or lycra body suits; however, the neck, face, and lips are still vulnerable. When a diver surfaces after a night dive, the snorkel should be checked to ensure that there are no tentacles attached that could sting the mouth and lips. In geographic areas where box jellyfish occur, swimmers should use bathing areas protected by "stinger fences" constructed to exclude box jellyfish and wear protective clothing to ensure contact does not occur.

First aid treatment for box jellyfish stings is given on page 129.

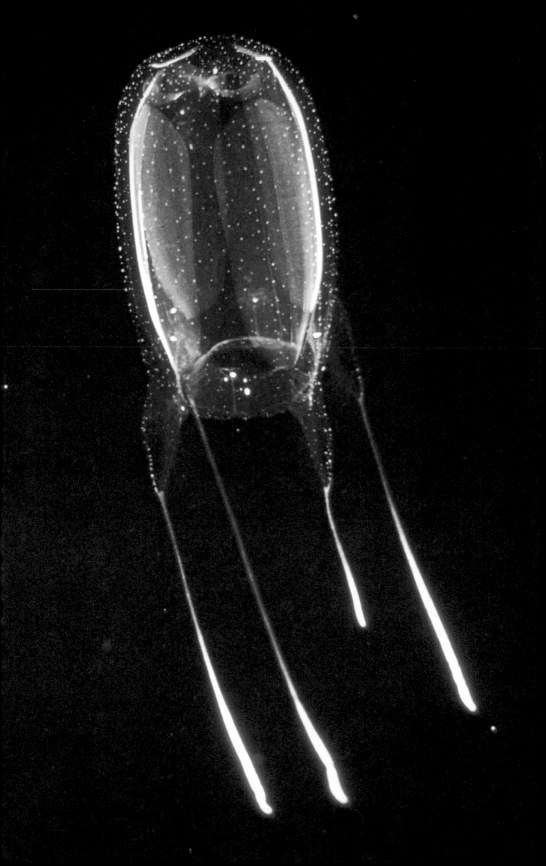

Sea Wasp (*Carybdea alata*)

Description. *Carybdea alata* represents one group of box jellyfish that is easily identified by its flattened four-sided bell with a single tentacle filament attached to the pedalium at each lower corner of the bell. The bell is 1 to 4 inches (2.5 to 10 cm) in height and up to 5 inches (13 cm) in width. The four pink tentacles can be contracted from a maximum length of 3 feet (1 cm) down to 3 to 4 inches (8 to 10 cm) in length. Rings of nematocysts cover the surface of each tentacle filament.

Range and Habitat. Sea wasps are found in warm coastal waters throughout the Atlantic and Caribbean. Usually encountered at night within a few feet of the surface, large swarms of this box jellyfish are attracted to lights or indirectly to the larval fish that lights attract. Sea wasps are strong swimmers able to travel 20 feet per minute (6 m per minute). They propel themselves by rapid pulsations of the bell as they search for the larval fish on which they feed. The appearance of this sea wasp seems to be influenced by wave conditions and lunar cycles.

Related Species. A larger subspecies *Carybdea alata grandis* is widely distributed in the tropical Indo-Pacific region. The rectangular-shaped bell is 9 inches (23 cm) in height and 5 inches (13 cm) in width. The

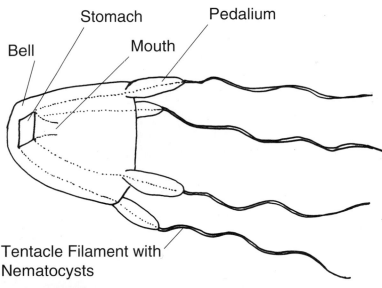

Structure of a box jellyfish.

◀ *The sea wasp is attracted to light, so divers should be extra cautious on a night dive. Photograph by Paul Humann.*

fleshy pedalia are 2 inches (5 cm) long, each with a single trailing tentacle and nematocyst clusters may or may not be present on the surface of the bell.

Hazard to Humans. MODERATE TO SEVERE. Even minor stings from contact with as little as ⅜ inch (1 cm) of tentacle cause intense pain and a welt with surrounding redness of the skin. Tightness in the chest may occur, which usually subsides within 30 minutes. Major envenomations can be serious and result in severe pain, respiratory distress, cardiac arrest, and coma. No permanent scarring of the skin has been reported for the sea wasp.

Raston's Box Jellyfish (*Carybdea rastoni*)

Description. This is one of the smaller box jellyfish species and is commonly called a jimble in Australia. The translucent box-shaped bell is only 1⅜ inches (3.5 cm) high and 1 to 1¼ inches (2.5 to 3.0 cm) wide. Depending on the extent of contraction, the four tentacles (one on each pedalium) are 2 to 12 inches (5 to 30 cm) long. Tentacles may be whitish, light blue, violet, or pink in color, and are more easily seen than the bell. This species is a miniature version of the sea wasp, *Carybdea alata*.

Swimming enclosures along the Queensland coast provide some protection from large box jellyfish; however, small species or juveniles are not completely excluded from these bathing areas. Photograph by Paul Goetz.

Range and Habitat. Jimbles are found in southwestern and western Australia and along the Queensland Coast, particularly during the summer (November through March), and in Japan, the Philippines, Hawaii, and other parts of the Indo-Pacific region. This species is frequently seen in quiet bays, often over sandy areas. Individual jimbles cluster close to the bottom during bright daylight hours, but ascend to feed near the surface at sunset, during the night, and on cloudy overcast days. Jimbles may be encountered in large swarms during certain seasons.

Hazard to Humans. SEVERE. Victims will experience immediate pain upon contact with the tentacles, which gradually fades to a stinging or itching sensation. Up to four red welts from the four tentacles may be produced on the skin. Tentacle sting marks on the victim's skin have a characteristic 90° bend tracing out a portion of the box-like shape. Welts are generally ¼ to ⅜ inches (0.5 to 1 cm) across and may persist for 1 to 2 hours; however, skin discoloration may persist for several weeks. Severe stings may be painful for up to 12 hours with the welts persisting for weeks and skin discoloration lasting for several months. Permanent scarring of the skin does not usually occur.

Irukandji Stinger (*Carukia barnesi*)

Description. This thimble-sized box jellyfish is one of the smallest species. The translucent box-shaped bell is 1 inch (2.5 cm) high and ¾ inches (2 cm) wide. The four tentacles (one on each pedalium) are highly contractile, ranging from 1½ inches (4 cm) to over 40 inches (1 m) in length, and have a hair-like structure. This species is similar in appearance to *Carybdea rastoni*. Nematocysts are concentrated in tiny red raised warts on the dorsal surface of the bell and in bead-like clusters on the tentacles. This stinger's name is taken from an aboriginal tribe near Cairns, Australia, where the species was first identified.

Range and Habitat. Irukandji stingers are widely found in tropical waters of the Indo-Pacific region including Australia, north to Indonesia and west to Fiji. However, this box jellyfish may be just one species within a group of several closely related species. In the Cairns area, this stinger is common during the summer months (November through February), but closer to the equator it is present from October through April.

Hazard to Humans. SEVERE. Initial pain is usually severe enough to prompt the victim to leave the water; however, the delayed onset of general symptoms can be hazardous for the victim. Pain first increases for several minutes after a sting and then diminishes over the next 30 minutes.

Small reddish bumps appear almost immediately on the affected skin, but then subside and are replaced with a red discoloration that may persist for up to three hours. Because the initial symptoms abate shortly after the sting, victims are sometimes convinced that all serious effects are over. This can lead to serious consequences if the victim returns to the water prior to the onset of the more serious general symptoms. General symptoms include acute abdominal pain (rigidity of the abdominal wall), chest and back pains, aches and pain in the limbs, vomiting, severe headaches, and difficulty in breathing. These general effects are not life-threatening, but hospitalization is recommended for treating the severe pain experienced by the victim. Symptoms may last for up to 12 hours and some ill effects may persist for several days. No deaths have been reported and no permanent skin scarring occurs. **NOTE:** Many of the general symptoms may be confused with decompression sickness (bends) if a diver has been stung during a dive. Additionally, the victim may experience general weakness, have difficulty in breathing, exhibit profuse sweating, nausea, and vomiting.

Flecker's Box Jellyfish (*Chironex fleckeri*)

Description. This species is the largest and by far the most deadly of all box jellyfish. Since 1900, this species is credited with over 70 human deaths in tropical Australian waters alone, a fact that is not revealed in most travel brochures. The bell can be as big as a man's head and weigh up to 6 pounds (3.7 kg). More commonly, the box-shaped translucent bell is 4 to 7 inches (10 to 18 cm) in height and 4 to 6 inches (10 to 15 cm) in width. At each corner of the bell, the pedalium branches into 15 tentacle filaments and each tentacle may be 6½ feet (2 m) long. The ribbon-like tentacles are bluish in color if the animal is undisturbed and become white or pale yellow when contracted. A ladder-like pattern of nematocysts on the tentacles leaves a corresponding pattern on the victim's skin. This box jellyfish possesses tentacles that are longer and more heavily armed with stinging cells than any other box jellyfish species. It has been estimated that an average-sized Flecker's box jellyfish possesses 5 billion nematocysts on its tentacles and is capable of injecting 100 to 200 times more venom into a victim than is injected by the similarly sized and closely related species, *Chiropsalmus quadrigatus*. This species is a fast swimmer that can swim at speeds up to 5 feet per second (1.5 m/sec) over short distances and can change direction abruptly to avoid predators such as sea turtles or to avoid turbulent waters. Four highly developed eyes, one on each side of the bell, provide the box jellyfish with good visual perception.

Chironex fleckeri *is the deadliest of all box jellyfish species, and a severe sting can be lethal to an adult in less than 5 minutes. Photograph by Keith Gillett, World Life Research Institute.* ▶

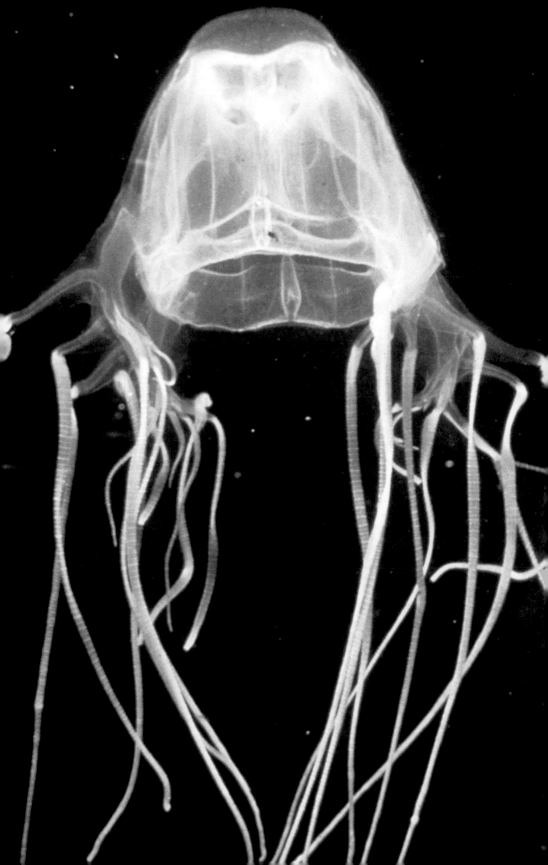

Range and Habitat. This species is widely distributed in the Indo-Pacific region. It has been reported in tropical waters from the east, north, and west coasts of Australia (north of the Tropic of Capricorn), and from Southeast Asia including the Philippines, Singapore, New Guinea, Borneo, and the Solomon Islands. Flecker's box jellyfish is typically found in muddy inshore coastal waters, especially in areas near the mouths of estuaries where adults spawn in the late summer and then die. Their progeny grow and mature in the estuaries throughout the fall and winter, until the following spring. Box jellyfish first appear in the estuaries as swimming larvae that settle on a hard substrate and develop into a sessile polyp stage. It is from this attached polyp stage that the box jellyfish then undergoes metamorphosis into a box-shaped medusa stage and leaves the estuary before the monsoon rains begin. In Australian waters, large adults and very small juveniles have been found during November (late spring). Juveniles mature in about four months, so the largest concentration of mature box jellyfish is found at the end of the summer (late March or early April).

Hazard to Humans. VERY SEVERE TO LETHAL. Children swimming in shallow water areas are the most frequent victims. The severity of the envenomation depends on the length of tentacle that comes in contact with the victim's skin (amount of venom injected), the size and body weight of the victim, thickness of the skin in the area of contact, size of the box jellyfish, and the time that has elapsed since the nematocysts were last fired. The venom of this species attacks the human body in three distinct ways: by causing severe skin death that results in permanent scarring of the skin, by destroying blood vessels, and by producing muscle spasms so severe that the heart muscle cannot relax and refill with blood before the next beat. It is this last characteristic of the venom that accounts for its lethality. Although an antivenom has been developed and is widely available from physicians in the endemic areas of Australia, the onset of severe symptoms can result in death before the victim can be treated.

Prevention. The only means to ensure protection from an envenomation is to wear a full body wet suit or lycra body suit when entering the water for any reason. Several towns along the Queensland coast have installed special swimming enclosures called "stinger fences" at popular local beaches to reduce the chance of envenomations. These protected areas are enclosed with fences 10 feet (3 m) high constructed of chain-link mesh interwoven with wooden slats. The enclosures, however, may not completely prevent the entry of all box jellyfish species; therefore, even in these protected enclosures, the wearing of a wetsuit or lycra body suit is still recommended. Flecker's box jellyfish feeds primarily on red shrimp and small fish during the wet monsoon season. The appearance of red shrimp washed up on beaches should be taken as an indication that this deadly box jellyfish may also be in the vicinity.

Indo-Pacific Sea Wasp (*Chiropsalmus quadrigatus*)

Description. This sea wasp has often been confused with the more lethal *C. fleckeri* because of its similar appearance and habits. *C. quadrigatus* possesses a box-shaped bell 4 inches (10 cm) in height and 4 inches (10 cm) in width. At each corner of the bell, the pedalium branches into nine tentacle filaments that are shorter, thinner, and less heavily armed with nematocysts than those of *C. fleckeri*. Because this sea wasp's ribbon-like tentacles contain fewer stinging cells and are shorter and fewer in number than those of *C. fleckeri,* its stinging potential is less than 1 percent of its dangerous relative.

Range and Habitat. These sea wasps are widely distributed in the tropical Indo-Pacific region including tropical waters of Australia, the Maldive Islands, Philippines, New Guinea, Borneo, Malaysia, and the Solomon Islands. Especially prevalent during the Australian summer months (October to April), this species may be present year round in areas closer to the equator.

Related Species. A closely related sea wasp, *Chiropsalmus quadrumanus* is identical in size to *C. quadrigatus*. Transparent tentacle filaments of this species are cylindrical and are covered with bead-like nematocysts. This Western Atlantic sea wasp occurs from Cape Lookout, North Carolina into the Gulf of Mexico and as far south as Brazil. During the summer months, these sea wasps typically occur in warm coastal waters, but are occasionally found offshore in the Gulf Stream current.

Hazard to Humans. SEVERE. Small children are at greatest risk. Stings from small specimens involving up to 3 feet (1 m) of tentacle are relatively minor. More extensive stings may cause severe pain, and the victim may go into shock. Small blisters develop along the area of the sting, but only shallow tissue destruction occurs, so there is no permanent scarring. Brownish skin discoloration occurs in areas of tentacle contact, but generally dissipates within six months. The affected area may itch as long as the discoloration persists. No fatalities have been attributed to this box jellyfish species. Antivenom prepared for *C. fleckeri* is also effective in the treatment of severe *C. quadrigatus* stings.

Annelida
Segmented Worms

The phylum Annelida (segmented worms) contains the class Polychaeta that includes over 5,300 species of marine worms. Many marine worms are brightly colored in red, pink, green, or iridescent hues. The bodies of all polychaetes are composed of a head, a trunk that contains similar segments throughout, and a terminal segment. Each trunk segment has paired lateral sensory bristles and branching gill filaments.

Polychaetes are divided into two groups: the subclass **Errantia** contains mobile or burrowing worms, and the subclass **Sedentaria** contains sedentary worms that live in fixed burrows or tubes. Fire worms are mobile, while Christmas tree and feather duster worms are sedentary polychaetes. It is primarily members of the subclass Errantia that are venomous to humans.

Hazard to Humans. In the fire worms, the paired lateral appendages (parapodia) extending from each body segment are well developed. Fire worms have hollow needle-like bristles on each parapodium that are composed of calcium carbonate and contain venom. This venom is liberated from the bristles upon penetration of the victim's skin.

Prevention. Fire worms should never be handled without heavy rubber or neoprene gloves as the brittles can penetrate cloth gloves. Never rub any skin area with gloves that have been used to handle a fire worm as the detached bristles that break off and stick to the glove can be transferred to the skin.

First aid treatment for fire worm stings is given on pages 129 and 130.

Bearded Fire Worm (*Hermodice carunculata*)

Description. This species is one of the largest Atlantic polychaetes. Although the body is typically 6 inches (15 cm) long, specimens can attain a length of 12 inches (30 cm). In cross section, the body is squarish and the head, middle, and terminal segments are all of similar width. Body color is variable, ranging from red-orange to green to chocolate brown. On each body segment, fire worms possess reddish gills and bundles of retractable, white bristles. The needle-like bristles are the defensive arma-

This bearded fire worm has already erected its defensive needle-like bristles for protection against a curious diver. Photograph by Pat Cunningham.

ments used to sting predators. The bristle shaft is hollow and removal from the skin is difficult.

Range and Habitat. This species is found in Florida, the Gulf of Mexico, and throughout the Caribbean. Its preferred habitat includes shallow coral reef areas or turtle grass meadows from the low tide mark to a depth of 50 feet (15 m). These fire worms are commonly seen in the early morning or late afternoon crawling on hard coral heads, soft coral, fire coral, or anemones on which they feed.

Hazard to Humans. MODERATE TO SEVERE. Snorkelers and divers are most likely to encounter this fire worm. Beachcombers may occasionally find one washed up on shore with floating debris and fishermen may find them coiled around baited hooks. Physical contact with the bristles causes an immediate, burning sensation that may persist for several days.

Red-tipped fire worms are covered with numerous long, brittle spines that contain a potent venom. Photograph by Paul Humann.

Red-Tipped Fire Worm (*Chloeia viridis*)

Description. This tropical polychaete is one of the smaller fire worms, attaining a length of up to 5 inches (13 cm), but with a stout body 2 inches (5 cm) in width. Red-tipped fire worms have an elliptical body shape with the head and tail segments being much narrower than the middle body segments. Body coloration is highly variable and can be brown, pale green, mottled, or iridescent with a dark stripe down the middle of the back. Long white bristles are contained in large bundles on each body segment and are tipped with a conspicuous reddish spot.

Range and Habitat. In the Atlantic, this fire worm is found in Florida, the Bahamas, and the Caribbean; while in the Pacific, it is found from Mexico south to Panama. This species inhabits sand or mud bottoms in reef rubble areas from the low tide mark to a depth of 130 feet (40 m).

Related Species. A related species, the golden fire worm (*C. flava*) is common in the Indo-Pacific region and occupies a similar habitat. This fire worm attains a body length of 8 inches (20 cm). Body coloration is orange with a characteristic black spot down the middle of the back on each body segment.

Hazard to Humans. MODERATE TO SEVERE. Because it generally inhabits deep water, this species is usually encountered by divers or captured on a baited hook by fishermen.

Mollusca
Snails, Octopus, and Squids

Members of the phylum Mollusca encompass a wide variety of forms including chitons, tusk shells, bivalves, snails, octopus, and squid. Approximately 75,000 living species of mollusks have been identified, however, only members of two of the classes are potentially hazardous to man. These two groups include members of the class Gastropoda (snails) and members of the class Cephalopoda (octopus and squid). Both of these groups contain species that have caused human deaths.

Within the class **Gastropoda,** the family Conidae (cones) are a carnivorous family of snails that use a venomous tooth to harpoon their prey. Cones are primarily limited to tropical waters and the family is represented by a large number of Indo-Pacific species. Cones are easily recognized by their beautifully patterned ice-cream-cone shaped shells. These snails are nocturnal predators that feed on polychaete worms, snails, and small fishes.

Within the class **Cephalopoda,** the family Octopodidae (octopus) contains most of the shallow water octopus species that man encounters. Octopuses are carnivorous and typically hunt their prey at night. Most species are shy and gentle creatures and do not bite unless mistreated through rough handling, removed from the water, or threatened.

Gastropoda
Snails

The class Gastropoda contains the largest number of mollusk species. In addition to the snails, this class includes shell-less snails such as the sea hares, sea slugs, and nudibranchs. The only family within the class Gastropoda that contains venomous species is the family Conidae. Cones are exclusively marine snails, most commonly found in tropical or subtropical waters of both the Indo-Pacific and Atlantic regions. Approximately 500 species of cones have been identified worldwide; however, only about 26 species occur in the Atlantic, 36 species occur in the eastern Pacific (Gulf of California to Ecuador), and the greatest representation of species is in the tropical Indo-Pacific region.

The cone's envenomation apparatus is composed of a muscular venom bulb, a venom duct, a radular sac (for storage of the radula teeth), and muscular proboscis. The small radula teeth found in most snails have been modified into hollow, harpoon-shaped barbs in cones. This harpoon-shaped barb is filled with venom as the tooth matures in the radular sac. When the cone is hunting its prey, one radula tooth is passed from the radular sac into the pharynx to the buccal cavity (mouth), and is finally

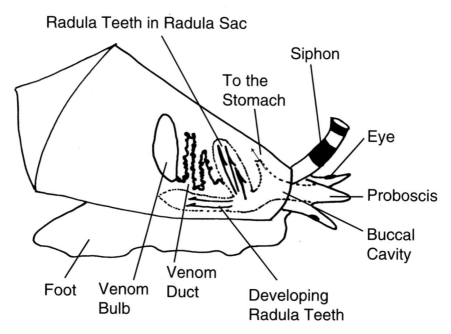

Envenomation apparatus of a cone.

The beautiful, glossy shell of the geographer cone has made it a prize for shell collectors, but it is the most deadly cone species in the Indo-Pacific region. Photograph by Paul Goetz.

passed to the tip of the proboscis. When prey come within range, the radula tooth is thrust from the muscular proboscis into the body wall of the prey. Venom is released into the wound upon penetration. The muscular venom bulb provides the force needed to move additional venom out of the venom duct, through the radular sac, into the buccal cavity and proboscis, and into the prey. Cone venom paralyzes the prey species.

Various species of cones have evolved to feed on worms (vermivores), snails or other mollusks (molluscivores), or on small fish (piscivores). The majority of cones are vermivores that feed primarily on polychaete worms. These cones have relatively small shells and possess simple or slightly serrated radula teeth that are often released after the prey is stung.

Molluscivores typically have large shells and possess large, heavily serrated radula teeth that are released after the prey is stung. The molluscan prey (primarily snails, including other cone species) are paralyzed quickly and are eaten in their shells. Digestive secretions passed from the proboscis into the prey assist in the digestion.

A small number of cones are piscivores. These species have the largest shells and possess large, elongated radula teeth. The teeth are almost an inch long (2 cm) with no serrations, but with a distinctive terminal barb. In the fish-eating cones, once the radula has been thrust into the fish, strong muscles at the tip of the proboscis hold the radula in place until the fish is completely paralyzed. This behavior is necessary so that the high-

At night, this geographer cone hunts small fish on which it preys. Photograph by Nancy Sefton.

ly mobile prey does not swim out of reach of the cone. Once subdued, the fish is swallowed through the proboscis, which may dilate up to one inch (2 cm) in diameter. Strong enzymes within the proboscis and buccal cavity assist in digesting the prey. Fish-eating cone species generally possess the most virulent venom as the toxin must quickly immobilize a fish. This is also the type of venom most likely to produce an adverse reaction in another vertebrate—man.

Hazard to Humans. Envenomations by Indo-Pacific cone species can result in death as no anti-venoms are currently available. The hollow radula tooth that is thrust into a victim's skin produces a puncture-type wound into which the venom is injected. Initial symptoms of a sting include localized pain and a burning sensation that is followed by numbness and a tingling sensation that can spread outward from the wound to involve the affected limb, and then the entire body. Often, victims experience tingling sensations in the lips, tongue, and mouth. More severe symptoms may follow including dizziness, nausea and vomiting, blurring of vision, difficulty in speaking and swallowing, paralysis, respiratory distress, coma, and death often resulting from cardiac arrest. Shell collectors are the primary victims of the venomous stings. Several Pacific cone

The five Indo-Pacific cones shown above are all considered hazardous to man and include (from top to bottom) the geographer cone, textile cone, cat cone, striated cone, and pearled cone. Photograph by Paul Goetz. ▶

species have caused human deaths, however, only two Atlantic cones, the crown cone (*C. regius*) and the alphabet cone (*C. spurius*) have been reported to have stung humans, but no deaths occurred. Reactions were reported to be comparable to a bee sting.

Prevention. Cones should never be handled without heavy gloves or collecting tongs. The older recommendation to hold the shell at the blunt end (spire end) is dangerous. Some species have the ability to extend their proboscis to reach that part of the shell and can successfully sting an unsuspecting victim. A cone shell should never be placed in your pocket or put inside a wetsuit or buoyancy compensator (BC) jacket because some species can sting through clothing.

First aid treatment for cone stings is given on page 130.

Geographer Cone (*Conus geographus*)

Description. The shell of this cone can attain a length of 6 inches (15 cm). Unlike the typical ice-cream-cone-shaped shell of most cones, the shell of the geographer cone is cylindrical. The thin, lightweight shell has a smooth surface and possesses a low spire. Exterior shell coloration is light pink with reddish-brown lines forming a matrix to encompass small triangular-shaped areas called tent patterns. Irregular bands of darker brown tent patterns curl around the body whorl. Interior shell color is white.

Range and Habitat. This highly venomous cone is widely distributed throughout the tropical Indo-Pacific region including Hawaii. This intertidal species is a nocturnal predator feeding primarily on small fishes. By day, it buries itself in sandy areas under pieces of coral rubble or coral ledges.

Hazard to Humans. SEVERE TO LETHAL. This species has been responsible for more human deaths and serious injuries than any other cone species. The venom contains several different toxins that have a variety of effects in humans. Some of the toxins act on skeletal muscles and some affect the central nervous system.

Striated Cone (*Conus striatus*)

Description. This large cone possesses a fairly heavy shell and may attain a length of 5 inches (12 cm). The shell has a flat spire (depressed below the shoulder) and the sides of the body whorl are curved. Shell coloration is pinkish with a pattern of large irregularly shaped brown blotches composed of closely spaced, parallel brown lines. Two irregular bands of darker blotches curve around the central portion of the body whorl.

Shell sculpturing includes fine parallel ridges that also curve around the body whorl becoming more pronounced toward the base.

Range and Habitat. This cone is widely distributed in the Indo-Pacific region from east Africa to northern Australia, Polynesia, and Hawaii. It occurs on shallow reefs and in moderately deep waters from 25 to 65 feet (8 to 20 m) deep. By day, this cone buries in the sand under pieces of coral rubble or ledges. By night, it is a fish-eating predator.

Hazard to Humans. SEVERE TO LETHAL. This cone has been responsible for several fatalities and severe injuries in humans.

Cat Cone (*Conus catus*)

Description. This small shell is robust and heavy, attaining a length of only 2 inches (5 cm). Exterior shell texturing is rough with grooves and ridges that curve around the body whorl and become more prominent basally. Exterior shell coloration is brown with irregular patches of pearly white that form radial bands along the length of the shell. These radial bands intersect two darker brown bands curving around the body whorl. Interior coloration is white with brown and white markings on the aperture lip.

Range and Habitat. This cone is widely distributed in the tropical Indo-Pacific region and is found from the Red Sea east to the Hawaiian Islands. Its preferred habitats include wave-washed intertidal reefs or rocky shores as well as subtidal areas where it hides in reef crevices by day. At night, this cone emerges to feed on small fish (e.g., gobies and blennies).

Hazard to Humans. MODERATE TO SEVERE. This species has caused minor human injuries; however, despite its small size, it is a fish-eating species, with potentially virulent venom, that should be handled with caution.

Textile Cone (*Conus textile*)

Description. This large thick-shelled cone can attain a length of 4 inches (10 cm). The smooth, glossy shell may assume a wide variety of shapes ranging from a slender body whorl with relatively straight sides to a shorter, squatter body whorl with highly curved bulging sides. The high shell spire is sharply pointed. Externally, the shell exhibits a tent pattern typical of many cones. The triangular white tents are outlined by axial bands of dark brown and discontinuous spiral bands of light yellow-brown. Interior shell coloration is white. Because the beautiful shell pattern resembles a richly colored fabric, the cone is also known as the cloth-of-gold cone.

Range and Habitat. This cone is widely distributed in the Indo-Pacific region. By day it hides under pieces of coral rubble or hides in sand pockets on reef platforms. This species also occurs in moderately deep water from 65 to 165 feet (20 to 50 m). It is a nocturnal predator of other mollusk species.

Hazard to Humans. SEVERE TO LETHAL. This cone has caused several deaths and severe injury to humans. The venom is thought to affect the central nervous system.

Pearled Cone (*Conus omaria*)

Description. This cone closely resembles the textile cone, but is smaller in size attaining a length of only 3 inches (8 cm). The shell is more slender in appearance with a needle-like top on the low spire. Externally, the white shell is covered with large areas of dark brown outlined tents. Two discontinuous, but wide brown spiral bands curve around the body whorl. Interiorly, shell coloration is white.

Range and Habitat. The pearled cone is widely distributed in the Indo-Pacific region. It inhabits shallow coral reef areas and offshore waters. This cone preys on other mollusks.

Hazard to Humans. MODERATE TO SEVERE. Pearled cone stings have caused severe symptoms in humans.

Cephalopoda
Octopus and Squids

There are approximately 650 species of cephalopods, including species of octopus, cuttlefish, and squid. These mollusks are highly advanced on the evolutionary scale, and have circular heads with highly developed eyes. The arms are located anteriorly and the visceral mass containing most internal organs is located posteriorly. While cuttlefish and squid can bite, these creatures rapidly propel themselves away from an overly curious diver if threatened. The slower moving octopus is often captured and handled by divers and thus has more opportunity to bite humans.

The envenomation apparatus of the octopus includes two pair of salivary glands that secrete venom via salivary ducts into the mouth cavity and a strong pair of chitinous jaws resembling an inverted parrot's beak. The beak is the formidable weapon used by the octopus to tear the flesh of its prey and is located ventrally at the center of the arms. Venom is introduced into the prey or victim at the time of the bite through the two small puncture wounds inflicted by the beak.

Hazard to Humans. Bites from most octopus species initially produce a tingling or burning sensation. The pain is first localized at the wound site, but later, severe pain may radiate outward to affect the entire extremity. Bleeding from the wound may be profuse because some species secrete anticoagulants in their salivary secretions, and swelling and redness of the wound area commonly occur. Other symptoms include an intense itching at the wound site, numbness of the mouth, lips, and tongue, blurring of vision, dizziness, vomiting, and difficulty in swallowing and speaking.

Bites from several blue-ringed octopus species that inhabit the Indo-Pacific region are far more serious and have resulted in the rapid onset of death (less than 5 minutes) in cases of human envenomations. Bites from blue-ringed octopus species initially can be painless. The only evidence that a victim has been bitten may be the presence of blood spots at the wound site or two small puncture wounds on the victim's skin. However, within several minutes, the onset of serious symptoms occurs. Typically, numbness or a tingling sensation is felt in the lips and tongue, and there is the rapid onset of respiratory difficulties, blurring of vision, dizziness, nausea and vomiting, difficulty in swallowing or speaking, general muscular weakness, and loss of motor control that can progress to complete paralysis. The venom is a potent neurotoxin that specifically causes paralysis of the respiratory muscles; consequently, the victim often dies from respiratory failure if suitable respiratory support cannot be obtained immediately. Respiratory support must be provided for as long as eight hours or until the victim's own respiratory functions return to normal.

Prevention. All octopus bites are potentially hazardous to humans, but can easily be avoided. Octopus are shy creatures that can be handled safely if a gentle touch is used. They pose no threat to divers or reef walkers unless provoked by careless or rough handling or if they are removed from the water. However, to prevent the possibility of a bite, never handle any octopus without heavy gloves. **For all blue-ringed octopus species, additional precautions should be taken to avoid being bitten.** Do not handle or allow any blue-ringed octopus species to come in contact with your body. Victims have been bitten even through thick clothing. These highly venomous species are best viewed at an aquarium or from a distance.

First aid treatment for blue-ringed octopus bites and for other octopus bites is given on pages 130 and 131.

Southern Blue-Ringed Octopus (*Hapalochlaena maculosa*)

Description. This tiny octopus has a body size of only 4 inches (10 cm) across from arm tip to arm tip. Its body and arms are mottled with bands of dark brown and ocher yellow which tends to camouflage it. Thin blue rings ⅛ inch (3 mm) in diameter are found only on the brown areas of the body and brown arm bands. When frightened, provoked, or removed from water, this species rapidly changes its appearance. Body coloration darkens and the fine light blue rings greatly enlarge in size and become a striking iridescent blue.

Range and Habitat. This temperate water octopus is common along the entire southern coast of Australia, north to Shark Bay in western Australia, and north to Victoria on Australia's east coast. This species inhabits both rocky areas with high wave action and sheltered sea grass meadows from the intertidal area to a depth of 30 feet (9 m).

Hazard to Humans. SEVERE TO LETHAL. Very small specimens are of less hazard than adults; however, children often find these octopus while playing in tide pools and because of a child's smaller body size, they are at greater risk. Death can result before medical assistance can be obtained for the victim.

Prevention. Never allow this species to come in contact with your body.

The southern blue-ringed octopus is a diminutive, but highly venomous species whose bite can cause death in humans within a few minutes. Photograph by Neville Coleman.

Northern Blue-Ringed Octopus (*Hapalochlaena lunulata*)

Description. This tropical species is approximately twice the size of its southern relative with a body size of 8 inches (20 cm) across from arm tip to arm tip. Because of its shy nature and ability to camouflage itself, this species is difficult to find. The body is a tannish yellow and both the body and arms are dotted by numerous large open rings. The center of each ring is an area of tan skin surrounded by a thin middle ring of iridescent blue and an outer slightly wider ring of black skin. These ring patterns can be as large as ⅜ inch (1 cm) in diameter. When alarmed, the blue rings become more prominent.

Range and Habitat. This species is found in all tropical waters of Australia including both the east and west coasts and throughout the tropical Indo-Pacific region. The preferred habitats include reef flats and shallow tide pools. Taxonomy of all blue-ringed octopus species needs further study. Some taxonomists believe a cluster of several separate, but closely related species occurs in the Indo-Pacific region.

Hazard to Humans. SEVERE TO LETHAL. See Hazard to Humans for the related species, the Southern Blue-Ringed Octopus on page 72.

Prevention. Never allow this species to come in contact with your body.

When alarmed, the electric blue rings on the body of the northern blue-ringed octopus enlarge in size giving a warning to predators and humans. Photograph by Carl Roessler.

Common Atlantic Octopus (*Octopus vulgaris*)

Description. Possessing a radial arm span of up to 6 feet (2 m), this octopus is the largest and most commonly encountered of the Atlantic species. The longest pair of arms is 3 feet (1 m) and is four times the body length. The first pair of arms is shortest. This species exhibits great variability in skin texture and coloration. Skin texture of the body and arms is a reticulated pattern of thin brown or black grooves, and body coloration is often reddish to brownish with scattered white spots or mottling. Adults are recognized by the deep brown to black grooves on their skin surface and by small white skin patches between their eyes.

Range and Habitat. In the western Atlantic, this octopus ranges from Connecticut to Florida, the Bahamas, and throughout the Caribbean, while in the eastern Atlantic, it ranges along the northern coast of Europe and into the Mediterranean Sea. This common species is found in coral reef areas, sea grass meadows, or on underwater wreckage at depths up to 75 feet (23 m). Unlike most other octopuses, this species is typically seen on coral reefs during daylight hours.

Hazard to Humans. SLIGHT TO MODERATE. See general discussion of Hazard to Health on page 71.

This common Atlantic octopus uses a threat display to frighten off an approaching diver. Photograph by Paul Goetz.

Caribbean Reef Octopus *(Octopus briareus)*

Description. This octopus species is smaller than the common Atlantic octopus and has a maximum arm length of 1½ feet (46 cm). The longest pair of arms is approximately five times the body length, and the third pair of arms is longest. External coloration ranges from pale pink to iridescent blue-green hues with red mottling. A distinguishing species characteristic is the presence of a dark brown ring around the eye. This species has relatively smooth skin with a few scattered pimple-like warts.

Range and Habitat. This octopus is distributed from North Carolina, south to Florida, the Bahamas, and throughout the Caribbean. It is a relatively common intertidal and shallow water species found under coral heads or in tidal pools at depths up to 75 feet (23 m). It is the most frequently encountered species on Caribbean coral reefs, but is generally only active at night.

Hazard to Humans. SLIGHT TO MODERATE. See general discussion of Hazard to Humans on page 71.

At night, the iridescent blue-green body color of the Caribbean reef octopus is most striking when the animal swims into the beam of a diver's underwater light. Photograph by Nancy Sefton.

Atlantic Pygmy Octopus (*Octopus joubini*)

Description. The Atlantic pygmy octopus is one of the smaller Atlantic species, with an arm span of only 6 inches (15 cm). The short arms are two to three times the body length and are all of relatively equal length. The skin on the upper body surface and arms is smooth. Body and arm coloration are highly variable and may be tan, red, brown, gray, or black.

Range and Habitat. This octopus is found in southern Florida, the Bahamas, and throughout the Caribbean. Its preferred habitat includes sand or mud bottom areas adjacent to reefs from the low tide mark to a depth of 35 feet (10 m). This octopus frequently inhabits empty shells or bottles.

Related Species. Two small related species include the seaweed (*O. hummelincki*) and brownstripe octopus (*O. burryi*). The seaweed octopus has an arm length of 6 inches (15 cm) and is found in the Florida Keys, West Indies, and south to Brazil. The brownstripe octopus has an arm length of 10 inches (25 cm) and is found in Bermuda, Florida, the Bahamas, the Caribbean, and in the Gulf of Mexico.

Hazard to Humans. MODERATE. Although small, this species is reported to have a virulent bite. Aquarium collectors are most often bitten. See general discussion of Hazard to Humans on page 71.

Echinodermata
Sea Stars, Sea Urchins, Sea Cucumbers

The phylum Echinodermata represents a diverse, exclusively marine group of animals. The most striking characteristic of these bottom dwelling creatures is their pentamerous radial symmetry—the body is divided into five parts arranged around a central axis. All echinoderms possess an internal skeleton composed of calcareous ossicles (plates). Typically, spines or tubercles project from the body surface, hence, the name echinoderm, which means spiny skin. Members of this phylum also possess a unique water vascular system. Tube feet are the external part of this internal hydraulic system of fluid-filled canals. Muscular contractions control water pressure in this system so that the tube feet may be contracted or extended enabling the animal to move. Generally terminating in suction tips, tube feet function in locomotion, feeding, and respiration.

Five distinct classes of echinoderms have evolved: **Asteroidea** or sea stars (1,600 species), **Crinoidea** or crinoids (550), **Ophiuroidea** or brittle and basket stars (2,000 species), **Echinoidea** or sea urchins, heart urchins and sand dollars (900 species), and **Holothuroidea** or sea cucumbers (900 species). Members of the Asteroidea and Echinoidea contain most of the species that are venomous to humans, while members of the class Holothuroidea contain species that produce secretions toxic to humans.

Asteroidea
Sea Stars

Members of the class Asteroidea were originally known as starfish; however, the name sea star is far more appropriate because this group is in no way related to the fishes. The asteroid body resembles a flattened star, usually with five stout arms or in multiples of five radiating out from the central body disc. In some species, broken arms can be regenerated, while other species actually reproduce asexually by detaching an arm that then develops into a new individual.

The dorsal or aboral surface of a sea star's arm has spines characteristic of the species as well as a reddish eyespot at the tip. The dorsal surface of the central disc contains the anus in the center and the madreporite, which is the entrance to the animal's water vascular system. The ventral or oral surface contains the mouth at the center of the body disc. Either two or four rows of tube feet extend from the mouth in an open groove down to the tip of each arm. The tube feet are the external projections of the water vascular system and are tipped with suction discs that assist the animal in respiration, locomotion, and in capturing prey. Sea stars have the ability to evert their gastric tissue out through their mouth to completely envelop and digest their prey external to the body.

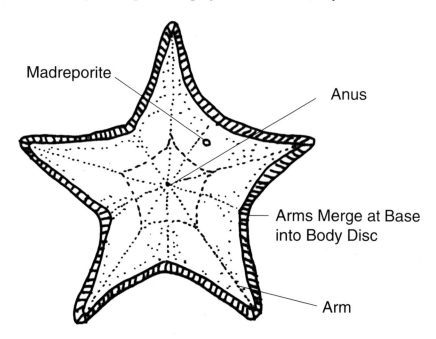

Madreporite

Anus

Arms Merge at Base
into Body Disc

Arm

Body structure of a sea star.

Crown of thorns sea stars are voracious predators of living coral, and explosions in their numbers have devastated many Indo-Pacific coral reefs. Photograph by Carl Roessler.

Hazard to Humans. The greatest hazard to humans comes from being punctured by the sharp spines. Venom is introduced into these wounds at penetration and fragments of the spines are often brittle and difficult to remove completely from the wound site. Secondary bacterial infections are an associated problem for these types of puncture wounds.

Prevention. Care should be taken to avoid contact with the spines. Wetsuits and heavy gloves generally provide adequate protection.

First aid treatment for crown of thorns sea star envenomations is given on page 132.

Crown of Thorns Sea Star (*Acanthaster planci*)

Description. Unlike most sea stars that are typically pentamerous, this large sea star may have up to 23 arms, although 13 to 18 arms are more commonly observed. The number of arms increases with increasing body size. The body disc is up to 16 inches (40 cm), but can attain 24 inches (60 cm) across. Body coloration can be blue, green, or grayish with the spines tinted with red or orange. This reddish-orange coloration is most striking when the respiratory papulae are expanded. The papulae are reddish finger-like extensions of the inner body wall that project out through pores in the surface of the disc between the spines. The upper surface and margins of the body disc and arms are covered with a soft skin and stout, hinged spines each terminating in a 3-sided blade at its tip. Each spine is composed of magnesium-rich calcite. The spines are typically 1 inch (2.5 cm) long, but can be up to 2½ inches (6 cm) in larger individuals and readily break off in wounds. The skin covering each spine is thick and contains two distinct types of cells that secrete both venom and mucus.

Range and Habitat. The crown of thorns is distributed widely throughout the tropical and subtropical coral reef areas of the Indian Ocean, Red Sea, Pacific Ocean including Australia, Melanesia, Micronesia, Polynesia, and Hawaii. Shallow sheltered lagoons and the leeward side of coral reefs are their preferred habitat. This sea star is found from the low tide mark to 90 feet (27 m) and, on windward reefs, they are usually found in deeper water away from areas of high wave action. Feeding exclusively on living coral polyps, crown of thorns prefer prey such as branching and plate corals rather than mounding or encrusting corals. Being nocturnal, this sea star takes refuge under coral ledges or in crevices by day and forages on the reef at night. In areas where their numbers have reached plague proportions (more than 15 adults per square yard or more than 18 per m^2), this species may be seen feeding both day and night. An adult sea star feeds by pushing its gastric sac out through its mouth. The gastric sac is a membranous material that when fully extended can cover an area larger than the animal's disc. As the everted gastric sac membrane covers the coral polyps, digestive fluids are secreted to dissolve the fleshy polyps into strings of tissue that can be absorbed. The sea star usually digests an area about half the size of its own disc. During an eight-hour period, all of the living coral polyps covered by the gastric sac will be killed and absorbed. One adult can consume polyps over an area as big as its body disc in a 24-hour period or eat over 5 square yards (4 square meters) of coral in a year.

Related Species. Ellis' crown of thorns sea star (*Acanthaster ellisii*), a related eastern Pacific species, has from 10 to 15 short, spiny arms covered with sharply pointed dorsal spines. The body disc is up to 18 inches

(46 cm) across. This sea star inhabits shallow reefs with an abundance of soft and hard corals to depths of 80 feet (24 cm). Ellis' crown of thorns ranges from the Gulf of California south to Peru.

Hazard to Humans. MODERATE TO SEVERE. This species' color and cryptic behavior enable it to blend well with its background on the reef so that snorkelers and divers may unwittingly come in contact with its sharp spines. Contact with the mucus secretions can produce contact dermatitis. Penetration of the skin by the long spines covered by venom-producing tissues causes the venom to be released into the wound area. Localized pain can be immediate and intense with swelling, redness, and numbness of the site. Victims may suffer symptoms such as repeated vomiting (every few hours for several days) and headaches when the envenomation is severe (more than 10 spines). Lymph glands in the groin and armpits may become tender and swollen if a secondary infection develops. If the spine tips break off in the wound, symptoms and complications may continue for weeks or months after the injury. Abscesses may form at the site of embedded spines and surgical removal may be required.

Prevention. Care should be taken when reef walking because this sea star can occur in very shallow water. Even dead animals washed up on the shore are capable of causing severe pain if tread upon with bare feet. Reef walkers, beachcombers, and swimmers should be careful where they step and wear appropriate foot protection. Even wetsuits and heavy gloves do not provide complete protection from the sharp spines. Divers on night dives should take particular care because this sea star is most active at night. This is one species to observe from a distance.

Penetration of the skin by several crown of thorns spines can cause acute pain, swelling, a protracted period of vomiting, and general weakness in the unlucky victim. Photograph by Nancy Sefton.

Echinoidea
Sea Urchins

The class Echinoidea contains the sea urchins, heart urchins, and sand dollars that are mobile echinoderms covered by spines of varying shape and length. Unlike the sea stars, sea urchins do not possess arms because the body plates (ossicles) are fused to form a solid case or test. The test of most sea urchins is spherical, while other members of the class such as the heart urchins and sand dollars have dome-shaped or flattened disc-shaped tests. The anus is located on the dorsal surface of the test. Radiating from the test are movable spines that can be tilted in the direction of an approaching predator. The spines of some species are needle-like projections more than a foot long, while others are short and stout with rounded tips. Sea urchins have long tube feet equipped with suction discs that are arranged in five pairs of rows that extend longitudinally on the test from the anus to the mouth. To clean the external surface of the test, urchins also possess three-jawed pincer-like structures with poison glands called pedicellariae. Like the sea stars, the mouth is located ventrally; however, the sea urchins have evolved an arrangement of five teeth in a jaw-like structure called Aristotle's Lantern. This specialized feeding structure is used in scraping algae from the substrate and can be protruded from the mouth for feeding. Tube feet in the vicinity of the mouth are long and allow the urchin to pull its mouth close to the substrate for feeding.

Hazard to Humans. The greatest hazard results from puncture wounds caused by the sharp spines and from pedicellaria envenomations. Venom is introduced into the wound at spine penetration and fragments of the spines are often brittle and difficult to remove completely from the wound. Secondary bacterial infections are often associated with these types of wounds. In addition to the spines, there is also a risk of being envenomated by pedicellariae. These pincer-like jaws can bite into the skin and venom is injected in the process. Fatalities have resulted from pedicellaria envenomations from some species.

Prevention. Care should be taken to avoid contact with the pedicellariae and spines. Wetsuits and heavy gloves provide adequate protection from the pedicellariae; however, they do not provide protection from the spines of all species.

First aid treatment for sea urchin spine or pedicellaria envenomations is given on page 133.

Long-Spined Sea Urchin (*Diadema antillarum*)

Description. The spheroid-shaped test of this urchin is up to 4 inches (10 cm) in diameter with spines up to 12 inches (30 cm) long. The test may be black or dark purple. In young individuals, spines may be white or black-and-white striped, but usually become uniformly black as the urchin matures. These spines are extremely sharp and can easily penetrate the skin and even a ⅜-inch (9-mm) wetsuit. Because the spines are extremely brittle in structure they are almost impossible to remove. Each spine is coated with a glandular layer of cells that secretes a venomous fluid.

Range and Habitat. This species is found in Florida, Bermuda, throughout the Caribbean, and south to Brazil in shallow coral reef areas at depths up to 130 feet (40 m). By day, these sea urchins hide in reef crevices; however, at night, they leave the protection of the reef to forage on algae in nearby eel and turtle grass meadows. During the 1970s, this sea urchin was extremely abundant in the Caribbean; however, its numbers have been reduced dramatically. A disease outbreak is attributed with causing the sharp population decline of these sea urchins.

Related Species. Three related species in the genus *Diadema* occur widely in the Indo-Pacific region. Palmer's needle-spined urchin (*D. palmeri*) is an inhabitant of temperate and subtropical rock reefs. The test is 4 inches (10 cm) in diameter with spines 4 inches (10 cm) long. The test and spines are bright red. Savigny's needle-spined urchin (*D. savignyi*), inhabit tropical and subtropical coral reefs, and has a test 4 inches (10 cm) in diameter with spines 5 inches (13 cm) long. This predominantly blue-black urchin sometimes has white markings on the test and spines. The largest of the three urchins is the diadem needle-spined urchin (*D. setosum*), an inhabitant of both tropical and subtropical waters. This species is most like its Caribbean relative having a test 4 inches (10 cm) in diameter with spines up to 15 inches (38 cm) long. In this species, the test and spines are predominantly blue-black.

Hazard to Humans. MODERATE TO SEVERE. Upon penetration, the brittle spines break off and remain embedded in the skin. Venom is released into the wound producing an immediate throbbing pain that may persist for several hours. Because embedded spine fragments dissolve slowly, the healing process may be prolonged. The wound may change color from a purplish-red to red, then to green, and yellow as the dark purplish spine pigments are slowly dissolved. In addition to the soreness and irritation the spines produce, there can be serious problems resulting from secondary bacterial infections. In severe cases, partial paralysis of the limbs and irregularities in pulse rate have been reported. This species is a

The 12-inch spines of the long-spined sea urchins present an impressive defense against predators and divers alike. Photograph by Paul Goetz.

hazard to divers, particularly during night dives in shallow areas where surge may carry a diver into contact with these urchins. Swimmers entering shallow water may also step on these urchins whose spines can penetrate tennis shoes.

Prevention. Divers often come into contact with this species when diving in areas of high surge and at low tide. When planning a night dive, divers should select sites where wave conditions and depth are appropriate. Vigilance is the best way to prevent contact with these urchins. Swimmers should be careful when entering or leaving the water in areas where this species is common.

Variable Sea Urchin (*Asthenosoma varium*)

Description. This large, short-spined sea urchin possesses a test of up to 7 inches (18 cm) in diameter. Coloration of the test is highly variable, but may exhibit alternating red, purple, brown, or black patterns. This urchin's thin test collapses when the animal is removed from water, giving the urchin a flattened beret-like appearance. Longer primary spines project beyond the densely packed secondary spines that cover the dorsal surface. The needle-sharp secondary spines are each tipped with a balloon-like skin sheath that covers a venom-filled sac. The sheath of muscle and connective tissue is often pale in color at the base with purple bands shading to electric blue at the tip. The highly venomous secondary spines, while fairly short, are thin and extremely sharp, and are able to penetrate most types of gloves. The venom is released when the spine penetrates the skin and breaks off in the wound.

Range and Habitat. This nocturnal sea urchin inhabits coral reefs, reef slopes, drop-offs, and coral outcrops in channels and between patch reefs throughout the Indo-Pacific region. It is found from the low tide mark to 200 feet (60 m).

Hazard to Humans. MODERATE TO SEVERE. The potent venom produces immediate and excruciating pain that can continue for many hours. In severe envenomations, swelling and pain can be so severe as to preclude normal use of an affected limb for up to a week. Divers are most at risk from contacts with this species on night dives.

The spines of the variable sea urchin are tipped with white balloon-like venom sacs that release the venom when the spine penetrates the skin. Photograph by Carl Roessler.

Flower Sea Urchin (*Toxopneustes pileolus*)

Description. The dome-shaped test can be up to 6 inches (15 cm) in diameter, but is typically 2 to 4 inches (5 to 10 cm) and is often covered aborally with pieces of algae, shell, and coral fragments. Aboral spines are up to ⅜ inch (9 mm) long, while the oral spines are up to ½ inch (12 mm) long. The spines are moderately robust and taper to a point. Flower sea urchins are found in shades of white, green, or red or bands of all three colors. The spines are almost completely concealed by the open flower-like globiferous pedicellariae up to ⅛ inch (3 mm) across. Each globiferous pedicellaria possesses a venom gland and three sharp fang-like teeth at the end of the jaws. When stimulated, sensory hairs on the inside of the jaws trigger the jaws to close and venom is injected through the fangs.

The fang-like pedicellariae, rather than the spines, are the main envenomating structures of the flower sea urchin. Photograph by Neville Coleman.

Pedicellariae cannot bite through the thick skin on the palm of the hand, but can penetrate the webbing between the fingers.

Range and Habitat. Flower sea urchins are found from east Africa to Japan, Australia, and Polynesia. This urchin occurs in tropical coral reef areas and sea grass meadows from the intertidal zone to 100 feet (30 m).

Related Species. The flower urchin (*Toxopneustes roseus*) has a domed-shaped test typically 5 inches (13 cm) in diameter covered by short spines and long, petal-shaped pedicellariae. This urchin is found on shallow eastern Pacific reefs from the Gulf of California south to Equador including offshore islands.

Hazard to Humans. SEVERE TO LETHAL. The venom disrupts normal nerve-muscle conduction resulting in muscle paralysis. Immediate and severe pain results that can last for several hours. Victims may collapse and experience paralysis of the eyelids, lips, tongue, and limbs, as well as respiratory distress. Deaths have been reported in some Asian countries.

Holothuroidea
Sea Cucumbers

The body form of this echinoderm class has evolved to resemble a cucumber with a mouth and feeding tentacles located at one end and an anus located at the opposite end. Because sea cucumbers generally lie on one surface, the tube feet used in locomotion are generally more highly developed on the ventral sole, and the dorsal tube feet are often reduced or almost absent. Body shape can vary from a rigid cylinder or spheroid shape to a flexible, elongated worm-like form. Sea cucumbers trap food particles on their mucus-covered tentacles and then transfer the food particles to their mouth.

The translucent tube feet of this sea cucumber are characteristic of echinoderms. Photograph by Pat Cunningham.

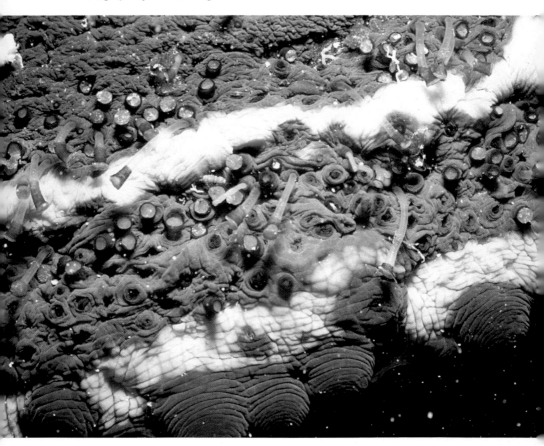

Hazard to Humans. Several species in the genera *Holothuria,* *Actinopyga,* and *Stichopus* are capable of expelling sticky tubules from their anus as a defensive mechanism. These sea cucumbers possess a mass of white, pink, or red tubules called Cuvierian tubules that are attached just inside the anus. When attacked by a predator or handled by a diver, the sea cucumber contracts the body wall expelling the tubules. These tubules are sticky, often disarming the attack by a predator. These ejected parts are regenerated over time. The tubules release a chemical called holothurin that is also found in the body wall. Mucus secretions on a sea cucumber's skin can be both a skin and eye irritant.

Prevention. Gloves provide adequate protection from contact with the mucus and sticky tubules. Those who handle sea cucumbers should avoid touching their skin or eyes until they have washed their hands thoroughly.

First aid treatment for sea cucumber contacts is given on page 131.

West Indian Sea Cucumber (*Actinopyga agassizi*)

Description. This tropical species can attain a body length of 12 inches (30 cm) and a width of 3 inches (8 cm). Its body shape and leathery skin closely resemble a large cucumber. The warty dorsal surface is dark gray

The West Indian sea cucumber hosts the pearlfish in its intestines. When predators approach, the pearlfish quickly swims into the anal opening of the sea cucumber for safety. Photograph by Paul Humann.

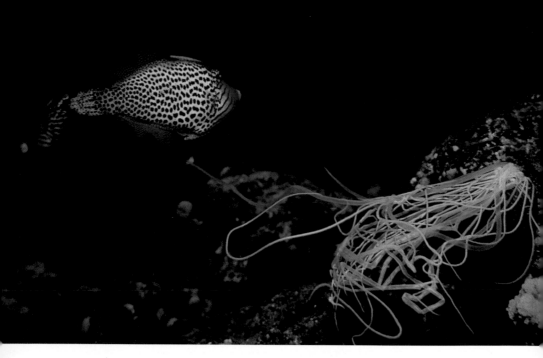

Expulsion of long, sticky Cuvierian tubules is a defense mechanism used by some sea cucumbers to thwart predators. Photograph by Paul Goetz.

or brown and white mottled and is clearly delineated from the paler ventral sole. The sole has three longitudinal rows of transparent, yellow tube feet, which allow the animal to creep slowly over the bottom. Five squarish anal teeth are visible when the animal exhales, and it is sometimes called the five-toothed sea cucumber.

Range and Habitat. This sea cucumber is commonly found associated with sea grass meadows or on sandy reef flats in Florida, the Bahamas, and the Caribbean. It can occur from the low tide mark to a depth of 90 feet (27 m).

Related Species. The leopard sea cucumber (*Bohadschia argus*) is a widely distributed Indo-Pacific species that plays host to a pearlfish just like its Caribbean counterpart, *A. agassizi*, and expels Cuvierian tubules to disarm predators. This species is easily identified by distinctive eye-shaped markings scattered over its body. This sea cucumber can attain 16 inches (40 cm) in length and is just one of a large number of species that proliferates in reef areas of the tropical Indo-Pacific region.

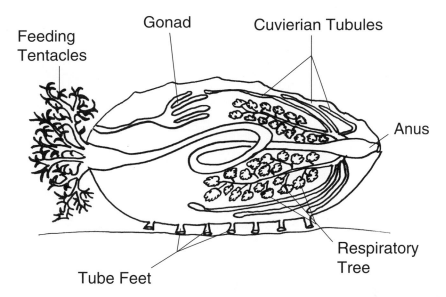

Feeding
Tentacles

Gonad

Cuvierian Tubules

Anus

Respiratory
Tree

Tube Feet

Body structure of a sea cucumber.

Hazard to Humans. SLIGHT TO MODERATE. The toxic substance, holothurin, is released from the animal's skin or the Cuvierian tubules after they are ejected from the body. Divers and snorkelers should avoid handling this species unless gloves are worn, because the toxic secretions can be irritating to the skin and to the eyes.

Chordata
Sharks, Stingrays, Bony Fishes, Sea Snakes

The phylum Chordata contains the vertebrate animals including the fishes, amphibians, reptiles, birds, and mammals. Of the vertebrates, only members of the fishes and reptiles contain venomous marine species. Fishes are the most ancient vertebrate members of the phylum Chordata, having first appeared in the fossil record some 400 million years ago. The fishes can be divided into two major classes: the Chondrichthyes, which includes the cartilaginous jawed fishes (sharks, skates, and stingrays) and the Osteichthyes, which includes all of the bony fishes. There are approximately 700 species of venomous fish worldwide. These include approximately 100 species of stingrays and 350 species of scorpionfish of the family Scorpaenidae, which includes scorpionfish, firefish, zebrafish (sometimes called lionfish), waspfish and stonefish. The remaining venomous fish species include several smaller families within the Osteichthyes.

Chondrichthyes. The more primitive class Chondrichthyes includes 550 fish species that are almost exclusively marine inhabitants. In this group, the internal skeleton is composed entirely of cartilage, and bone is completely absent. Members of this ancient group generally have five to seven pairs of gill slits that open separately to the outside, skin that is covered with placoid scales giving it a sandpaper-like texture, and numerous teeth. Stingrays form the largest number of venomous species within this class and their defensive arsenal includes one or more venomous spines located on their muscular tail.

Osteichthyes. In the more highly evolved class Osteichthyes, members have a skeleton of bone strengthened with calcium carbonate, a single gill cover or operculum protecting the gills, and scales that partially or completely cover the body or are completely absent. This evolutionarily successful class includes 20,000 fish species that have radiated into a wide variety of freshwater, estuarine, and marine habitats. Scorpionfish are the predominant venomous marine species within this class, although a number of different families have also evolved envenomating spines associated with various parts of the body. The defensive arsenal of scorpionfish includes spines associated with the dorsal, anal, and pelvic fins. Other prominent families of venomous fish species include stargazers, eel-tailed catfish, sea catfish, rabbitfish, and weeverfish. Members of these other families possess spines associated with a variety of fins that may include the dorsal, anal, pelvic or pectoral fins or shoulder spines hidden behind the operculum. These families will not be discussed in great detail in this guide because many of these species are not often encountered by man.

Reptilia. The class Reptilia includes approximately 6,500 species of turtles, crocodiles, lizards, and snakes. Of these species, however, there are only about 50 venomous marine species that include the Indo-Pacific sea snakes. Sea snakes consist of two groups: the family Hydrophiidae or true sea snakes and the family Laticaudidae or sea kraits. Like their closest relatives the terrestrial cobras and kraits, sea snakes have fixed fangs and highly potent venom. Sea snake venom is a complex mixture of proteins that is produced and stored in venom glands in the posterior portion of the head. Venom flows via ducts into hollow fangs located in the snake's upper jaw.

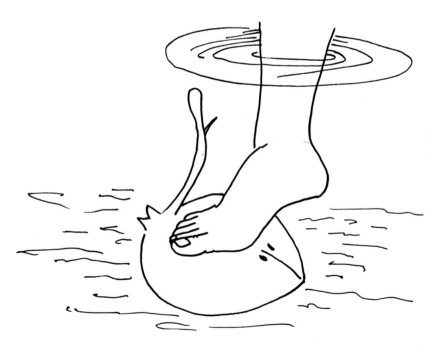

The pressure of a human foot on the back of a stingray will cause the ray to thrust its tail forward causing stings primarily to the foot, ankle, and calf.

Chondrichthyes
Sharks and Stingrays

Stingrays are by far the most important group of venomous marine fishes within the class Chondrichthyes. There are two superfamilies within this class that contain the majority of venomous stingray species: the superfamilies Dasyatoidea (105 species) and Myliobatoidea (41 species). The superfamily Dasyatoidea consists of two large families, the Dasyatidae (whiptail stingrays and freshwater river stingrays), which contains 70 species, and the Urolophidae (round stingrays or stingarees), which contains 35 species. The superfamily Myliobatoidea consists of two small families: the Gymnuridae (butterfly rays), which contains 12 species, and the Myliobatidae (eagle ray, bat rays, and cownose rays), which contains 29 species.

Because of both their pleasant and disastrous interactions with humans, the dasyatid stingrays are much better known than their myliobatid relatives. On the pleasant side, diving among the dasyatid rays at Stingray City off Grand Cayman Island in the Bahamas is a popular activity. At this site, large numbers of southern stingrays, attracted to a shallow sandy area in the expectation of an easy meal, allow divers to swim among them and touch them. On the unpleasant side, however, the dasyatid rays are notorious for causing the majority of venomous marine fish stings to man. Along the Atlantic coast and in the Caribbean region, the major venomous fishes to be reckoned with include less than two dozen species of stingrays. However, these stingrays are responsible for 750–1500 envenomations annually. For comparison, a comparable number of scorpionfish species in the same geographic area cause an estimated 300 envenomations annually. The total number of envenomations is probably much higher because statistics are based only on the number of individuals seeking medical attention. Divers, snorkelers, reef walkers, swimmers, and fishermen are all at risk from these stingrays. Stingrays are responsible for the majority of marine envenomations because they inhabit the shallow coastal waters that are also frequented by man. Many of these species conceal themselves by lying partially buried in the sediment. Because of this, they are often stepped on by unsuspecting beach goers who must endure the painful consequences.

Members of the other superfamily Myliobatoidea are also a hazard to humans because they too possess venomous tail spines. However, these rays generally swim in midwater and only feed on the bottom. Because

Divers at Stingray City off Grand Cayman Island enjoy touching these graceful animals but must be careful not to inadvertently step on the stingrays. Photograph by Nancy Sefton. ▶

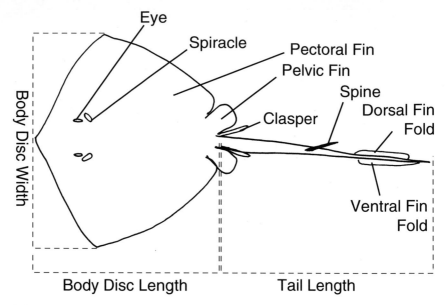

Major body structures of stingrays.

they are less likely to bury themselves in the sand and because the musculature associated with their tail is less well-developed than the dasyatid stingrays, they are less efficient at using their spine defensively. However, they are still potentially dangerous to fishermen who may hook them or net them while trawling.

Hazard to Humans. Stingrays use one or more large spines or stings on the dorsal surface of the tail as defensive weapons. Each serrated spine is covered by a layer of venom-secreting tissues. Venom secreted from glands along the grooves on either side of the spine flows into the wound. The pressure of a human foot on the dorsal surface of a stingray causes the animal to thrust its tail forward and upward, thus inflicting a deep laceration or puncture-type wound to the foot, ankle, or calf of its victim. A number of fatalities have resulted from the physical damage inflicted by the powerful tail and the resultant blood loss caused by the spine. Most of the victims are swimmers or fishermen wading in shallow water close to shore.

In addition to the pain associated with the physical damage from spine penetration, there is additional pain associated with release of venom into the wound. Envenomation by a stingray generally produces a sharp shooting pain within 10 to 15 minutes. Victims may exhibit one or more of the following symptoms: reduction in blood pressure, vomiting, diarrhea, sweating, rapid heart beat, or muscular paralysis. Deaths have been reported from envenomations when the victim was stung on the torso or neck region. In addition to tissue damage, blood loss, and pain resulting from the entry of the spine, severe secondary infections often accompany a sting even if the wound is properly cleaned. It is extremely important that the victim see a physician to ensure that the wound site has been properly cleaned and that secondary infections are treated promptly. A tetanus prophylaxis is also advisable.

Prevention. To prevent contact, swimmers and waders should shuffle their feet to frighten a stingray into deeper water. Reef walkers should use a walking stick to probe the sand in front of them. Fishermen should use the utmost care when removing a stingray from a fishing line or untangling it from fishing gear. Vigilance is the best way to prevent contact.

First aid treatment for stingray and venomous fish stings is given on page 133 and 134.

Southern Stingray (*Dasyatis americana*)

Description. This dasyatid stingray has a kite-shaped body disc that can attain a wingspan of 5 feet (1.5 m) and a length of 6 feet (1.8 m) from head to tail. The head is not well-defined. Dorsal body coloration is variable, ranging from gray to dark brown with a lighter ventral surface. A row of tubercles runs along the midline of the back from the head to the base of the tail. One venomous spine is located dorsally about half way between the base and the tip of the long tail.

Range and Habitat. This stingray ranges from New Jersey south to Brazil; however, it is most common in the Caribbean and throughout the Gulf of Mexico.

Related Species. Three related western Atlantic species include the bluntnosed stingray (*D. sayi*), which has a 3-feet (1-m) wingspan and ranges from New Jersey to Brazil, the Atlantic stingray (*D. sabina*), which has a 1-½ foot (45-cm) wingspan and ranges from Virginia to Brazil, and the roughtail stingray (*D. centroura*), which has a 8- to 12-feet (2.4-to 3.7-m) wingspan and ranges from Cape Cod to Florida. Many more species in this cosmopolitan genus occur in the Indo-Pacific region.

Hazard to Humans. SEVERE TO LETHAL. Because the tail is muscular and the spine is located between the base and the tip of the tail, this stingray can inflict a well-directed sting. This species is a hazard to swimmers, waders, divers, and fishermen.

The venomous stinger of the southern stingray is clearly visible half way along the dorsal surface of the tail. Photograph by Paul Goetz.

Marbled Ribbontail Ray (*Taeniura melanospilos*)

Description. This large stingray has a roundish body disc that can attain a width of 5½ feet (1.7 m) and a disc length of 4½ feet (1.4 m). The head is not well-defined. Dorsal coloration is medium to dark gray with a black marbling pattern. Ventral coloration is white. The tail is slightly longer than the length of the disc and has one venomous spine. This species is also called the black-blotched stingray.

Range and Habitat. This species ranges widely in the Indo-Pacific region from the Red Sea to the eastern Pacific region around the Galapagos Islands and Cocos Island. This ray inhabits waters from 10 to 1650 feet (3 to 500 m) deep, but is generally encountered in lagoons, on rocky slopes, or coral reef areas. Like most stingrays, it is a bottom feeder preying on a wide variety of mollusks, crustaceans, and benthic fishes. Divers may encounter solitary individuals or large aggregations of this stingray.

Related Species. The blue spotted fantail ray (*T. lymma*) is a related species widely distributed in the Indo-Pacific region from East Africa

The marbled ribbontail ray is a common sight at Cocos Island in the eastern Pacific Ocean. Photograph by Nancy Sefton.

through the western Pacific. It is frequently seen by divers on the Great Barrier Reef. Dorsal body coloration is tan with numerous electric blue spots scattered on the disc surface. Two venomous spines are located on the mid portion of the tail.

Hazard to Humans. MODERATE TO SEVERE. See general discussion of Hazard to Humans of stingrays on pages 96 and 97.

Yellow Stingray (*Urolophus jamaicensis*)

Description. The body disc is nearly round, being slightly longer than it is wide and attaining a total length of 2.5 feet (76 cm). A distinctive dark spotted pattern appears on the yellowish dorsal surface of the disc. The muscular tail is shorter than the length of the disc and has a caudal fin at the end. One venomous spine is located near the tip of the tail.

Range and Habitat. This stingray is most commonly found from Florida south through the Caribbean area including the Yucatan Peninsula and the island of Trinidad. It is an inshore bottom-feeding predator of mollusks.

Cryptic body coloration of a yellow stingray makes it difficult to see even in clear water. Photograph by Paul Goetz.

Related Species. Three related species that are found in the Pacific Ocean include the round stingray (*U. halleri*), the banded stingaree (*U. cruciatus*), and the bullseye stingray (*U. concentricus*). The round stingray possesses a circular disc up to 22 inches (56 cm) in length that is gray or brown, often mottled with yellow spots or other markings. This species occurs from northern California to Panama over sand or mud bottoms from intertidal waters to a depth of 70 feet (21 m). In June, this species moves inshore to breed and females return to shallow waters again in August and September to spawn. It is during these times that they are most hazardous to swimmers, and they are occasionally hooked by shore and pier fishermen. The banded stingaree is a species common to the temperate waters of Australia from New South Wales south to Tasmania and west to southern Africa. The disc is longer than it is wide attaining a total length of 20 inches (50 cm). It is easy to identify this species by the series of dark cross-like markings on its lighter colored dorsal surface and its extremely short, thick tail with a single venomous spine. Often encountered by divers and swimmers, this stingray is also caught on hook and line or trawled by fishermen.

The bullseye stingray is a species common to the Gulf of California that displays striking dorsal markings similar to the banded stingaree. The disc is slightly longer than it is wide, with a disc width of up to 2 feet (0.6 m). The dark dorsal markings form concentric rings on the outer edge of the disc. This stingray prefers bays and shallow sandy areas around reefs.

Hazard to Humans. MODERATE TO SEVERE. This species is a hazard to swimmers, waders, divers, and fishermen. Contacts usually occur when the victim is entering or leaving the water because this species often conceals itself by lying half-buried in the sand. Because the tail is so muscular and the spine is located near the tip of the tail, this species is extremely dangerous to man because it can inflict a well-directed sting. There are reports that some Urolophidae species have been observed to swim backwards at the sight of a potential predator or threatening human and successfully implant their sting.

Spotted Eagle Ray (*Aetobatus narinari*)

Description. The body disc of this myliobatid ray has distinctive triangular-shaped pectoral fins. The protruding head is distinct from the body disc and the eyes and spiracles are located laterally on the head. In large individuals, the body disc can attain a wingspan of 11 feet (3.5 m), but 8 feet (2.4 m) is more typical. The body is almost two times wider than the length of the disc, and the long whiplike tail is 3.5 times longer than the body disc length. Dorsal skin coloration varies from gray to black to blue and contains numerous whitish or bluish spots of variable size and shape. Spotted patterns appear in juveniles, changing to a combination of rings and spots in adults. Two to five venomous spines are located at the base of the tail.

Range and Habitat. This is a cosmopolitan species that inhabits tropical and warm temperate inshore waters worldwide. Shellfish are the typical prey. Generally, only single individuals are observed; however, schools may be seen during spawning periods or migrations. This species is commonly seen around reef habitats, but is also frequently encountered in the open ocean.

Hazard to Humans. SLIGHT TO MODERATE. This species is a hazard primarily to fishermen who are stabbed by the spines while trying to remove the ray from a baited hook or other fishing gear. The location of the spines at the base of the tail and lack of muscular development of the tail make this species less likely to sting humans.

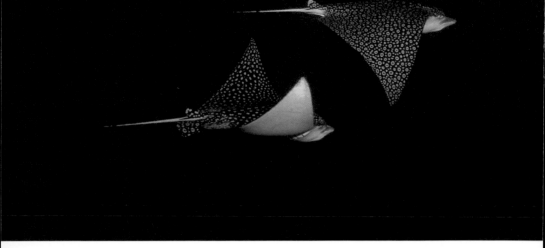

Fishermen are often stung while trying to free spotted eagle rays from their nets or fishing lines.

Only the outline of the lips of this spotted scorpionfish reveal the animal's well concealed position in the surrounding marine growth. Photograph by Paul Goetz.

Osteichthyes
Bony Fishes

Within the class Osteichthyes, scorpionfishes are the major group of venomous marine fishes that are potentially dangerous to humans. There are about two dozen species of scorpionfish that range from the temperate waters of the North Atlantic to the tropical Caribbean Sea, and account for an estimated 300 envenomations annually. As with the stingrays, a much more extensive and diversified representation of the family Scorpaenidae (scorpionfishes) occurs in the Indo-Pacific region. Most of the 350 scorpionfish species occur in the Indo-Pacific region with 80 species identified from Australian waters alone. Venom glands are associated with the dorsal, anal, and pelvic spines of this family. Although envenomations from scorpionfish can be painful, no deaths have been reported from the Atlantic and Caribbean species. This is not the case for stings by the more venomous Indo-Pacific species, such as the stonefish, that have caused human fatalities.

Several other families of venomous marine fishes within the class Osteichthyes are discussed briefly beginning on page 114.

Hazard to Humans. Most members of the family Scorpaenidae are masters of camouflage and often lie still in areas of marine growth thus becoming almost invisible to a passing diver. The greatest risk is that divers will be stung by brushing against these fish while they are concealed. Divers can also be stung if they inadvertently corner or threaten a scorpionfish thereby provoking an attack. Fishermen are at risk of being stung on the fingers and hands as they try to remove these fish from their lines or untangle them from nets. Reef walkers are at risk of stepping on some species that lie half-buried in shallow coastal waters.

Prevention. Divers should never provoke scorpionfish as they may lunge forward in self-defense with the venomous spines erected. Vigilance is a person's best protection for avoiding contact. Fishermen should always wear heavy gloves when removing a scorpionfish from a trawl or fishing line. Reef walkers should wear thick soled shoes and carry a walking stick to probe the sediment in front of them to frighten away any scorpionfish.

First aid treatment for stingray and venomous fish stings is given on pages 133 and 134.

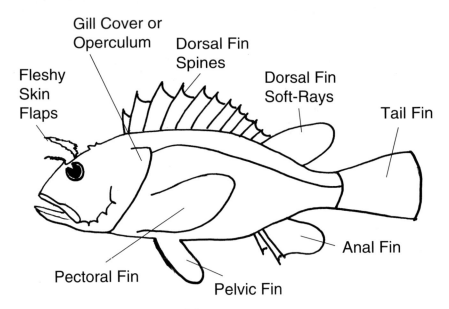

Gill Cover or
Operculum

Dorsal Fin
Spines

Dorsal Fin
Soft-Rays

Fleshy
Skin
Flaps

Tail Fin

Pectoral Fin

Pelvic Fin

Anal Fin

Major body structures of the bony fishes.

Spotted Scorpionfish (*Scorpaena plumieri*)

Description. Largest of the Atlantic species, the spotted scorpionfish can attain a maximum length of 17 inches (43 cm). This fish has a large head with numerous spines and a continuous dorsal fin composed of 12 venomous spines and 9 rays. The dorsal body surface is mottled with dark brown or black patches on a paler background. Numerous fleshy flaps covering both the head and body provide excellent camouflage. The light-colored tail has three distinctive dark vertical bars. In adults, the back side of the pectoral fin contains a large black area with striking white spots.

Range and Habitat. This fish inhabits shallow rocky or coral reef areas to a depth of 50 feet (15 m) and ranges from Cape Cod south to Brazil including Bermuda, the Caribbean, and the Gulf of Mexico. In the eastern Atlantic, it is found on St. Helena and Ascension Islands.

Hazard to Humans. SLIGHT TO MODERATE. The spotted scorpionfish is a master of camouflage. Divers and fishermen are most at risk from being stung. Fishermen are also at risk when removing this excellent eating fish from their lines or trawling gear.

The venomous dorsal spines of the plumed scorpionfish are erected for protection when the fish is threatened by a predator or provoked by a diver. Photograph by Paul Humann.

Plumed Scorpionfish (*Scorpaena grandicornis*)

Description. This common species of Atlantic scorpionfish attains a maximum length of only 7 inches (18 cm) and its body form is more laterally compressed than the spotted scorpionfish. The dorsal fin is continuous and is composed of 12 venomous spines and 9 rays. Its most striking characteristic is the long plumed tentacles located above its eyes. The tail is mottled brown with three vertical bars similar but less well defined than those seen in the spotted scorpionfish. This species is also known as the grass scorpionfish in some areas.

Range and Habitat. The plumed scorpionfish is commonly found in inshore areas, inhabiting sea grass meadows at depths up to 40 feet (12 m) in Bermuda, the Bahamas, southern Florida, and south along the coast through Central America to Brazil. This species is not commonly found on most Caribbean islands.

Hazard to Humans. SLIGHT TO MODERATE. This small scorpionfish, like other members of its family, is a master of camouflage. Divers and fisherman are most at risk from being stung.

Barbfish (*Scorpaenna brasiliensis*)

Description. This is one of the larger species of Atlantic scorpionfish, attaining a maximum length of 14 inches (36 cm). This robust fish is pinkish or reddish in color with lighter mottling and it usually has two brown body spots, one behind the gill cover and the other behind the pectoral fin. The dorsal fin is continuous and is composed of 12 venomous spines and 9 rays. The large head also contains numerous spines and long plumed tentacles above the eyes are well developed. Because the body is covered with numerous fleshy flaps of skin, it is difficult to distinguish this fish from the marine growth in which it often hides.

Range and Habitat. The barbfish ranges from Virginia south along the Atlantic Coast, into the Gulf of Mexico to Brazil but is less common in the West Indies. This species inhabits inshore waters over mud, sand, rocks, or coral to a depth of 300 feet (90 m). This is one of the most commonly seen species of scorpionfish especially along the south Florida coast.

Hazard to Humans. MODERATE TO SEVERE. This species is reported to be one of the most venomous of the Atlantic scorpionfish. Divers and fishermen are at greatest risk of being stung.

Well camouflaged by fleshy skin flaps, a barbfish lies motionless waiting for an unsuspecting prey. Photograph by Anne Dupont.

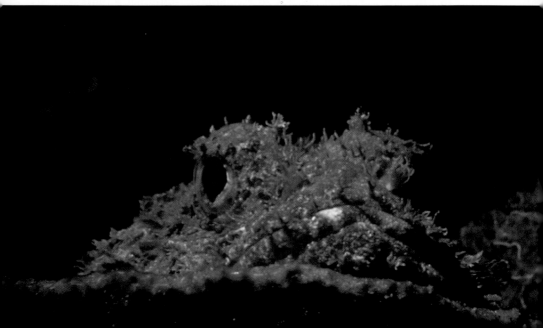

The California scorpionfish is the most venomous and one of the most common of the West Coast scorpionfish. Photograph by Howard Hall.

California Scorpionfish (*Scorpaena guttata*)

Description. This spiny, thick-bodied species is one of the larger scorpionfish ranging up to 17 inches (43 cm) in total body length. As with most scorpionfish, it has a large spiny head and highly variable body coloration ranging from a brick red to reddish brown to light brown. Numerous darker black and brown spots and blotches are commonly seen covering the body and fins. This species possesses 12 dorsal spines as well as spines on the anal and pelvic fins. All of these spines are venomous. The venom is produced in glands at the base of each spine and runs up to the tip through a groove in the spine.

Range and Habitat. This nocturnal species occurs along the Pacific Coast of North America from southern California south along Baja, California and into the Gulf of California. It prefers rocky or sandy shore areas and kelp beds from the low tide mark to 600 feet (180 m).

Hazard to Humans. MODERATE TO SEVERE. Contact with the venomous spines is immediately painful and the skin may become red and swollen. General symptoms of envenomation include nausea, diarrhea, vomiting, general fatigue, and headaches. Although stings from this species can be very painful, they have never been fatal. West Coast fishermen are at greatest risk because this is an excellent eating fish.

107

Smallscale Scorpionfish (*Scorpaenopsis oxycephala*)

Description. Body coloration of this scorpionfish can range from a mottled bright red to reddish brown color. The total body length can attain 12 inches (30 cm). The head, body, and fins are camouflaged with a covering of branching tentacles and skin flaps, and these are particularly well-developed on the head. The first dorsal spine is short and only half the length of the second and third spines.

Range and Habitat. This scorpionfish is widely distributed in the Indo-Pacific region from the coast of East Africa and the Red Sea, eastward through the Indian Ocean to the central Pacific. Its preferred habitat includes shallow coral reefs.

Related Species. A related species is the raggy scorpionfish (*Scorpaenopsis venosa*). Its dorsal spines gradually increase in length from the first to the third spine. Body coloration is brown, and the fins have dark spots arranged in rows. This smaller relative attains a total body length of only 7 inches (18 cm) and is found from the east coast of Africa through the Indian Ocean to the Central Pacific.

Hazard to Humans. MODERATE. See general discussion on Hazard to Humans of scorpionfish on page 103.

This smallscale scorpionfish stays close to the reef trying to conceal itself from potential prey. Photograph by Paul Goetz.

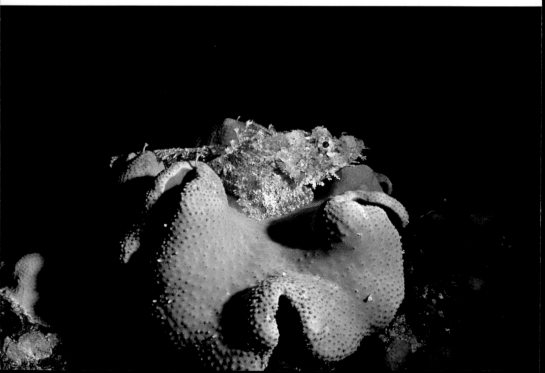

Leaf scorpionfish come in a wide array of colors—black, brown, red, and yellow. Here two color forms share the same reef. Photograph by Deb Fugitt.

Leaf Scorpionfish (*Taenianotus tricanthus*)

Description. This is one of the smaller scorpionfish with a total body length of only 4 inches (10 cm). The laterally compressed body has a sail-like dorsal fin that appears to be continuous with the caudal fin. Skin flaps are present above the eyes and the body scales have been modified to resemble small spiny bumps. Body coloration is highly variable, ranging from pale yellow to red, brown, or black, and may be mottled. Because it is a poor swimmer, this scorpionfish is often seen swaying from side to side in the current like a floating leaf.

Range and Habitat. Leaf scorpionfish are widely distributed in the Indo-Pacific region and have been reported from the coast of Africa, throughout the Indian and Pacific Oceans to Hawaii and the Galapagos Islands in the eastern Pacific. Its preferred habitat is the outer slope of coral reefs. In the past, these fish were erroneously thought to be quite rare.

Hazard to Humans. MODERATE TO SEVERE. Twelve dorsal spines are capable of injecting venom into the skin upon contact. Despite its diminutive size, this species possesses potent venom. (See the general discussion on the Hazard to Humans of scorpionfish on page 103).

The red firefish swims slowly above the reef extending its pectoral fins like a beautiful butterfly extending its wings. Photograph by Nancy Sefton.

Red Firefish (*Pterois volitans*)

Description. This graceful firefish can attain a total body length of 15 inches (38 cm). Body coloration exhibits a distinctive vertical banding pattern. Broad brown or black vertical bands alternate with narrower pink or white bands. Head coloration is similarly patterned. Fleshy tentacles above the eyes may be very long. The 13 venomous dorsal spines are long and well-developed. This species also has three anal fin spines and two pelvic fin spines. The outer half of the 13 to 15 unbranched pectoral fin rays are free with broad membranes giving a feathery appearance. Structural differences in the pectoral fins within this genus are used to identify different species. Other common names for this species include turkeyfish, butterfly cod, and lionfish.

Range and Habitat. Red firefish are distributed in the western Pacific region from western Australia and Malaysia, to southeastern Polynesia, and north to Japan. Its preferred habitat includes caves, ledges and overhangs in coral reef areas from 25 to 130 feet (8 to 40 m) deep. This species is most active just after dark.

Hazard to Humans. SEVERE. This venom produces excruciating pain for victims. Venom is produced in glands located in grooves on the front side of each spine. The glands have a thin skin covering or sheath. No venom duct is present. When threatened or provoked, this species may aggressively lunge forward with its long, feathery dorsal spines erect to sting its attacker.

Weedy Scorpionfish (*Rhinopias aphanes*)

Description. This well-camouflaged species has a large head that comprises almost one-third of its total body length of 10 inches (25 cm). The snout is upturned with an oblique mouth. A conspicuous white spot is located below the eye on the side of the jaw. The lower jaw, snout, occipital areas, and pectoral fins are covered with branched leafy tentacles. Skin flaps are also prominent along the sides of the body. Both the leafy tentacles and ragged skin flaps give the fish a cryptic appearance resembling weedy underwater growth thereby completely concealing its 12 venomous dorsal spines. Body coloration is highly variable, ranging from yellowish green to reddish brown to dark brown with a maze-like or scribbled pattern of darker markings.

Range and Habitat. This species is distributed from the northeast coast of Australia to New Caledonia, New Guinea, and northward to Japan. Weedy scorpionfish are stealthy predators that lie in wait for their prey by looking like a clump of seaweed. As the prey approaches, the fish engulfs it with powerful suction that it creates by quickly opening its mouth. This species occurs in coral reef areas at depths up to 100 feet (30 m).

A master of camouflage, the weedy scorpionfish can be easily overlooked by a diver in certain environmental settings. Photograph by Carl Roessler.

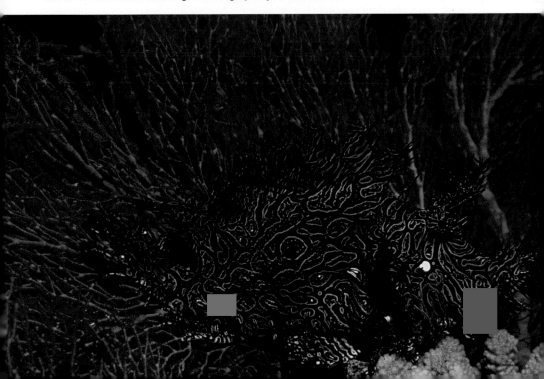

Hazard to Humans. MODERATE to SEVERE. Because it remains motionless for long periods and is so well camouflaged, this species is extremely difficult for a diver to see underwater particularly when it hides in areas covered by weedy growth. See general discussion on the Hazard to Humans of scorpionfish on page 103.)

Estuarine Stonefish (*Synanceia horrida*)

Description. Estuarine stonefish can attain 12 inches (30 cm) in body length. The eyes are elevated on the head with a prominent bony ridge running between and above the eyes. The light to dark brown body coloration is sometimes mottled. Large, raised warts are prominent on the sides of the body from the area behind each operculum to the base of the tail. The 13 highly venomous dorsal spines, three anal fin spines, and two pelvic spines are the primary envenomating structures. This species is also called the horrid stonefish.

Range and Habitat. This species is widely distributed in the Indo-Pacific region from Indian waters, south to Australia and north to China. It is commonly encountered in embayments, estuaries, and on offshore coral reefs at depths up to 130 feet (40 m).

The estuarine stonefish often lies half buried in sediment with only its spines, eyes, and mouth projecting from the sediment. Photograph by Carl Roessler.

Hazard to Humans. SEVERE TO LETHAL. This species typically lies half-buried in the sediment and is difficult to see. Beachcombers, reef walkers, and waders are at greatest risk. Stonefish venom is notorious for producing excruciating pain that may last several days. Stonefish spines are short and robust and the integumental sheath surrounding the spine is very thick. Two large venom glands are located on either side of the spine shaft, and a venom duct delivers the venom deep into the wound. Recovery from a severe sting may take several months.

Prevention. Beachcomber, reef walker, and waders need to be especially careful in shallow areas where this species occurs. Use of a walking stick to probe the bottom and wearing thick soled footwear can reduce contacts.

Reef Stonefish (*Synanceia verrucosa*)

Description. Reef stonefish can attain a body length of 14 inches (35 cm). The eyes are widely spaced with a deep depression between them that distinguishes this species from the estuarine stonefish. Body coloration is highly variable depending on the environmental surroundings of

This cryptically mottled reef stonefish closely resembles a piece of coral rubble from its surrounding habitat. Photograph by Paul Humann.

the fish. A master of camouflage, body coloration can range from a mottled gray to dark brown with scattered patches of reddish orange. The 13 highly venomous dorsal spines, three anal spines, and two pelvic spines are the primary envenomating structures.

Range and Habitat. This species is widely distributed in the Indo-Pacific region from the east coast of Africa to the Red Sea, and eastward to Australia and Polynesia. Reef stonefish inhabit coral reef areas and rubble bottom areas near bommies and often hide under rock outcroppings or ledges to depths up to 130 feet (40 m). This species often lies partially buried in the sand and blends in with its surroundings, particularly in coral rubble areas.

Hazard to Humans. SEVERE TO LETHAL. Stonefish venom is notorious for producing excruciating pain. Two large venom glands are located on either side of the spine shaft and a well-developed venom duct delivers the venom deep into the wound. Recovery from severe stings can take months.

Prevention. This species lies half-buried in the sediment and is difficult to see even when not buried. Beachcombers, reef walkers, and waders are at risk in coastal areas where this species occurs. Use of a walking stick to probe the bottom and wearing thick soled footwear can reduce contact. Divers are at risk of mistaking this fish for a piece of coral rubble.

Other Venomous Fishes

In addition to the estimated 350 species of scorpionfish that occur worldwide, there are several other smaller families within the class Osteichthyes that also possess venomous spines. Most prominent of these families are the stargazers, eel-tailed catfish, sea catfish, rabbitfish, and weeverfish. These groups will not be discussed in great detail as many are not often encountered by man.

Stargazers (family Uranoscopidae) include about 30 species of medium-sized fishes that inhabit all oceans. The majority of species are deep

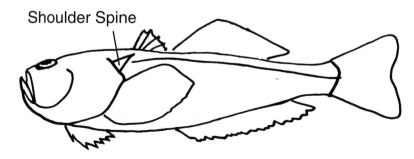

Shoulder Spine

Venomous spines of a stargazer.

water inhabitants that are not generally encountered by man, although a few species inhabit shallow subtidal areas. Underwater, stargazers are not easy to spot as they often remain buried with only their eyes and mouth exposed waiting for unsuspecting prey to approach. The envenomating apparatus includes a large shoulder spine behind each operculum. In addition, these fish are able to produce an electric shock from the area just behind the eyes.

Dorsal Fin Spine

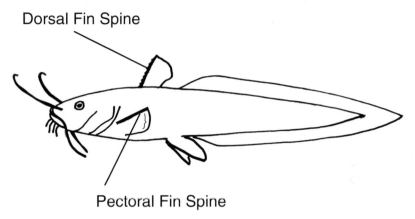

Pectoral Fin Spine

Venomous spines of the eel-tailed catfish.

Eel-tailed catfish (family Plotosidae) are confined to the tropical Indo-Pacific region with almost half of the 40 species occurring in freshwater rivers in New Guinea and Australia. The 20 marine species are typically inhabitants of coastal estuarine areas or coral reefs. Many species are recognized by their eel-shaped bodies, four pairs of chin barbels, and three prominent serrated, highly venomous spines. A single stout spine occurs in front of the dorsal fin and on each of the pectoral fins.

The related group of **Sea Catfish** (family Ariidae) possesses the characteristic catfish body with a deeply forked tail, typically three pair of chin barbels, and a prominent venomous spine in front of the soft-rayed portion of the dorsal fin and on each pectoral fin. Members of this tropical and subtropical family occur worldwide and include about 120 species. Two common Atlantic species include the hard head catfish (*Arius felis*) that ranges from North Carolina southward into the Gulf of Mexico to the Yucatan penisula and the gafftopsail catfish (*Bagre marinus*) that range from North Carolina southward into the Gulf of Mexico and south to Brazil.

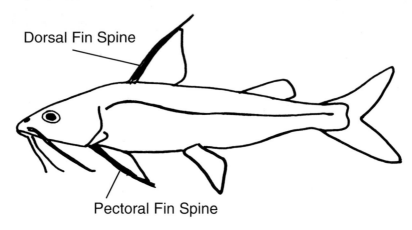

Dorsal Fin Spine

Pectoral Fin Spine

Venomous spines of a sea catfish.

There are 28 species of **Rabbitfish** (family Siganidae), an exclusively marine group of herbivore that is confined to the Indo-Pacific region. The envenomation apparatus includes 13 dorsal, 4 pelvic, and 7 anal fin spines. These fish are unique in that their pelvic fins possess a spine at each end with three fleshy soft rays in between. Rabbitfish are diurnal (active during the day), feeding primarily on benthic algae and sea grasses. Some species feed on tunicates and sponges. These fishes are often seen in pairs or tight schools over sea grass meadows. Many species are highly edible, and fishermen are most at risk from envenomation.

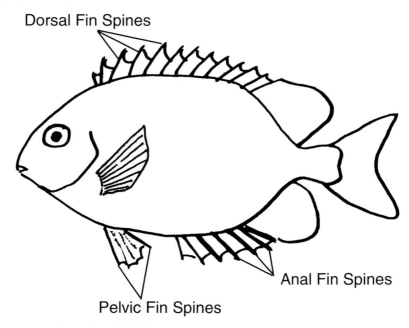

Dorsal Fin Spines

Anal Fin Spines

Pelvic Fin Spines

Venomous spines of a rabbitfish.

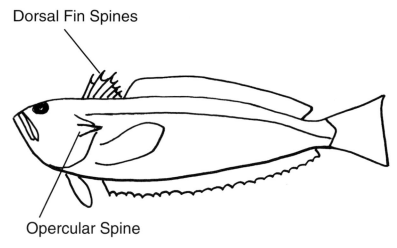

Dorsal Fin Spines

Opercular Spine

Venomous spines of a weeverfish.

Weeverfish (family Trachinidae) are small elongated marine fish generally less than 18 inches (46 cm) in total body length. Weevers are bottom-dwelling species that inhabit coastal bays and typically bury themselves in the sediment with only their heads exposed. The envenomating apparatus consists of five to seven slender spines in the dorsal fin and a dagger-like spine concealed behind each operculum. The venom of the weeverfishes acts as both a hemotoxin and a neurotoxin similar to sea snake venom. Represented by only four species, this group occurs along the eastern Atlantic Coast of Europe and Africa, and into the Mediterranean Sea.

Reptilia
Sea Snakes and Sea Kraits

Like sea turtles, marine iguanas, and saltwater crocodiles, sea snakes have successfully invaded the marine environment. Within the class Reptilia, the sea snakes are the only group of venomous marine animals and are by far the most successful of the marine reptiles with over 50 species identified in the Indo-Pacific region. Sea snakes range in size from less than 1½ feet (0.5 m) to almost 6 feet (1.8 m) in total body length. Like their closest relatives the terrestrial cobras and kraits (family Elapidae), sea snakes have fixed fangs and highly potent venom. The venom is injected into prey and human victims through hollow fangs located in the snake's upper jaw.

Sea snakes (family Hydrophiidae) and sea kraits (family Laticaudidae) are widely distributed in tropical and temperate waters of both the Indian and Pacific oceans. The major difference between these two families is that while true sea snakes live entirely at sea where they feed, rest, and bear live young, the amphibious sea kraits leave the sea to rest and lay their eggs. Sea snakes species are found from the east coast of Africa, into the Indian Ocean from the Arabian Sea to the Bay of Bengal, south along the Malay Peninsula to Australia, Tasmania, and New Zealand, north through the South China Sea to southern Japan and eastward to the Pacific coast of Central America from Mexico to Ecuador. Distribution of this predominantly tropical family is usually limited by water temperatures ranging from more than 68°F to less than 92°F (20°C to 33°C). The Atlantic Ocean, Mediterranean Sea, and Red Sea are devoid of any sea snake species.

Although only a small percentage of people bitten are actually envenomated by sea snakes, their venom is highly toxic and some species can produce enough venom in one bite to kill over 20 humans. Sea snakes are not generally dangerous, however, unless provoked to attack. Most species capture their prey (usually small fish) on or near the ocean bottom in relatively shallow coastal waters less than 160 feet deep (50 m). The broad continental shelf areas of northern Australia and the southeast Asian continent provide prime sea snake habitat. This region is characterized by vast expanses of shallow warm water that exhibits only slight seasonal temperature variations. Few sea snake species range beyond the continental shelves eastward of Australia to the Pacific islands. The 32 species found in Australian waters represent almost 60 percent of the total number of species distributed worldwide. The table that follows summarizes the number of sea snake species reported from various geographic areas of the Indo-Pacific.

Numbers of Sea Snakes Species By Area

Persian Gulf	9	Ryukyu Islands	8
West Coast of India Arabian Sea	14	Australia & New Guinea	32
East Coast of India Bay of Bengal	19	New Caledonia, New Hebrides, & Loyalty Islands	7
Burma, West Coast of Malay Peninsula, & Strait of Malacca	23	Solomon Islands & Bismarck Archipelago	5
Gulf of Thailand	22	Polynesia & Micronesia	5
South China Sea to the Formosa Strait	24	West Coast of Central America	1

Hazard to Humans. Sea snake envenomations generally occur on one of two areas of the body. Typically, waders or swimmers are bitten in the foot or leg when they accidentally step on a sea snake often in murky coastal waters. In contrast, fishermen are generally bitten on the fingers, hand, or arm while trying to release a sea snake from a net or line. Sea snake bites are inconspicuous, painless, and without swelling, which distinguishes them from venomous fish stings that may produce immediate and excruciating pain. Fang marks produced by sea snake bites may appear as one, two, or more small dots that are usually circular and similar in appearance to a hypodermic injection mark. Sometimes, the bite appears as small scratch marks. There is a surprisingly low incidence of serious poisoning from sea snakes relative to the lethality of their venom. Only about one-third of all victims bitten by sea snakes exhibit poisoning symptoms. These symptoms range from trivial to severe. Even before antivenom was available, only about 10 percent of those victims bitten actually died. However, to be prudent, all sea snake bites should be treated as life-threatening until the victim has been examined by a physician and the extent of the envenomation can be assessed.

It is important to remember and to remind bite victims that a lethal quantity of venom is rarely injected in most sea snakes bite incidents. Most victims suffer primarily from fright reactions that generally occur shortly after the bite. These symptoms may include cold and clammy feeling skin, rapid shallow breathing, a weak pulse, and may result in the victim collapsing.

If venom is injected into the wound, poisoning symptoms can be observed 30 minutes to four hours after the bite. In severe cases, clinical symptoms occur within two hours. Poisoning symptoms include muscular pain and stiffness when the victim tries to move, general body weakness, a dry feeling in the mouth, difficulty in swallowing and speaking, inability to open the mouth fully or sit up because of intense pain, constant thirst, periodic sweating, vomiting and headaches, and myoglobinuria (production of red-brown urine within 3 to 6 hours post-envenomation). Respiratory failure may occur within several hours of the bite. Victims may lapse into a coma and succumb to cardiac arrest or acute renal failure. Victims of fatal envenomations usually die within 24 hours after the bite. However, death should not occur if a victim receives adequate medical treatment within the first few hours after the bite.

Administration of antivenom is not a first-aid treatment. It is a medical procedure and should only be given by a qualified physician under hospital conditions. Antivenom that effectively neutralizes the venom of 11 species of sea snakes is available. Because adverse serum reactions can occur in a small number of patients, antivenom should only be given when systemic poisoning is clinically present. Antivenom has been successful in treating victims of mild envenomations even if administered 48 hours after the bite. Therefore, physicians have adequate time to identify those victims that clearly require antivenom treatment.

Prevention. Beachcombers, reef walkers, snorkelers, or swimmers should shuffle their feet in turbid water areas to frighten sea snakes away and should avoid swimming or wading in estuarine areas. While swimming on the surface, snorkelers and swimmers are not usually at great risk from being bitten because sea snakes are primarily bottom feeders. Fishermen should maintain a healthy respect for sea snakes. If a sea snake is hooked, the fishing line should be cut rather than trying to unhook the sea snake.

Attacks on divers are relatively rare; however, most sea snakes will bite in self-defense if provoked. Generally, sea snakes are curious and want to taste your body with their tongues as they swim in search of prey. A diver should try to remain as calm and as motionless as possible. Because many people have an aversion to snakes, this may be a difficult task. A leisurely swimming style is characteristic of a curious snake, whereas an attacking aggressive snake will swim rapidly with its head jerking from side to side. To fend off a curious sea snake, a diver may try interposing a fin between himself and the sea snake thus allowing the snake to taste the fin. This tactic may be sufficient to discourage the snake from investigating further, although because of their curious nature, they may repeatedly try to "taste" a diver. Never kick a sea snake away with your fins because this is certain to provoke an attack.

Sea snakes are very curious creatures and often approach and follow divers. Photograph by Deb Fugitt. ▶

Limited information suggests that attacks on divers and snorkelers may be most likely to occur during the mating season (May, June, and July) on the Great Barrier Reef and in the Coral Sea of Australia. If diving during this period, one source recommends that a diver carry a short length of dark rope (presumably resembling a sea snake) which could be dropped to momentarily divert a snake's attention. While the sea snake is temporarily occupied with the decoy sea snake, a diver can make a safe retreat. For divers, a ¼ inch (6 mm) wet suit appears to provide an adequate amount of protection from the bites of most sea snake species, especially when a full wet suit, hood, and gloves are worn.

First aid treatment for sea snake bites is given on pages 134 and 135.

Olive Sea Snake (*Aipysurus laevis*)

Description. One of seven species of sea snakes in the genus *Aipysurus,* the olive sea snake is a large, heavy-bodied snake. This sea snake is the largest member of its genus with an average body length of 4 feet (1.2 m), although individuals nearly 6½ feet (2 m) have been reported. Body col-

The olive sea snake is one of the most commonly seen species along the Great Barrier Reef. Photograph by Paul Humann.

oration and patterning are highly variable. Some individuals are a dark brown or purplish-blue brown dorsally and are pale brown ventrally. More commonly, the body may be dotted irregularly with numerous white scales or with dark scales. Tail coloration varies from dark brown to almost white, except for a dark brown dorsal ridge.

Range and Habitat. The olive sea snake is a very common species on the Great Barrier Reef in Australia, but its range also includes the Gulf of Carpentaria, Timor Sea, and Arafura Sea, and in New Guinea waters, the Gulf of Papua. Some eastern populations of this sea snake on reefs of the Coral Sea extend this species' range to New Caledonia. This sea snake is the most abundant species found associated with coral reefs.

Hazard to Humans. SEVERE TO LETHAL. See general description of sea snake hazard to humans on pages 119 and 120.

Yellow-Bellied Sea Snake (*Pelamis platurus*)

Description. This sea snake is rather small, having an average body length of only 2½ feet (0.7 m). The yellow-bellied sea snake has a unique body coloration pattern in which a dark brown or black dorsal coloration contrasts with a white, yellow, or pale brown ventral coloration. These

Unlike most sea snakes, the yellow-bellied sea snake waits at the surface among floating debris for small fish to swim within its reach. Photograph by Smithsonian: Carl Hansen.

*Unlike sea snakes that bear live young at sea, the banded sea kraits (*Laticauda sp.*) must return to land to lay their eggs. Photograph by Paul Humann.*

colors are sharply divided along the mid-lateral line of the body. The broad tail may be yellow with distinctive black spots or bar patterns. Although highly polychromatic, the pattern of coloration is atypical of most other sea snake species that exhibit banded, blotched, or uniform coloration patterns. An all yellow variety is found along the Costa Rican coast and Gulf of Panama.

Range and Habitat. A truly pelagic species, this sea snake's geographic distribution is more extensive than any other sea snake species. It occurs in tropical and warm temperate waters throughout the Indo-Pacific region from the east coast of Africa, through the Indian Ocean, to Australia, then north to Japan, and eastward to Micronesia, Polynesia, Melanesia, and to the Pacific Coast of Mexico south to Ecuador. It appears to need a minimum sea surface temperature of 68°F (20°C) to maintain a breeding population; however, individuals have been found washed ashore in areas north and south of its breeding range. Some individuals have washed ashore after storms in Southern California. Often found along drift lines (areas of convergence of two ocean currents), this species feeds primarily on juvenile fish attracted to the surface of these drift lines. Because of its pelagic nature, this sea snake may have migrated from the western Pacific via the Equatorial Counter Current. Unlike other sea snakes, it can be seen in large numbers at various water depths and distances from shore. Because it is a weak swimmer, it is propelled mostly by ocean currents and is often seen swimming slowly or resting at the surface. Coastal currents are often responsible for stranding this species on beaches where it is completely helpless.

Hazard to Humans. SEVERE TO LETHAL. This species is one of the most dangerous sea snake species because of the virulence of its venom and the quantity of venom produced. Despite this, there have been no reported bite incidents attributed to this sea snake in eastern Pacific coastal waters. Some bite incidents have been reported from African waters, but most deaths have occurred in Asian coastal waters particularly among fishermen. (See general description of sea snake Hazards to Humans on pages 119 and 120).

First Aid for Marine Envenomations

Step-by-step first aid procedures for the major groups of venomous and toxic marine animals are given below. These procedures are designed to reduce the quantity of venom introduced into the victim and to reduce pain. **It is important to note that first aid procedures are no substitute for receiving medical treatment from a qualified physician.**

Sponge Contacts

1. **Do not rub the area of contact** and never rub affected hands across the face or eyes.
2. Remove visible spicules from the skin as soon as possible with tweezers or by using a piece of adhesive tape to peel them off.
3. Soak the contact area with vinegar for up to 15 minutes, or 40% isopropyl alcohol for 5 minutes, by applying a large gauze pad or piece of cloth (e.g., T-shirt or washcloth) to the skin and dousing it liberally with vinegar or alcohol. Dry the skin thoroughly.
4. Apply 1% hydrocortisone lotion to the affected skin twice daily to reduce itching. Continue treatment until the irritation subsides.
5. If a severe skin rash, itching, swelling or pain persist, or an infection develops, contact a physician immediately as antibiotics may be required.

Coral Cuts

1. As soon as possible, scrub the wound with soap and water, then flush the wound liberally with fresh water to remove any polyp tissue or coral fragments. **Deep cuts or those with profuse bleeding require immediate medical attention by a physician.**
2. Apply hydrogen peroxide and allow the wound to bubble to remove additional coral fragments. Rewash the wound with fresh water. Apply an antiseptic (e.g., betadine) to the wound.
3. Apply bacitracin ointment and cover the wound with a sterile gauze pad or other sterile dressing. **Keep the wound dry.**
4. **Repeat Steps 1 through 3 twice daily.**
5. If pain and swelling persist or an infection develops, contact a physician immediately as antibiotics may be required.

6. Tetanus prophylaxis is advisable for the deep laceration-type wounds that may result from coral cuts.

Sea Anemone Stings

1. Remove any tentacles adhering to the skin by washing the skin with seawater. **Do not rub the contact area.**
2. Soak the contact area with vinegar for up to 15 minutes by applying a large gauze pad or piece of cloth (e.g., T-shirt or washcloth) to the skin and dousing it with vinegar. Dry the skin thoroughly. *Note: The use of meat tenderizer is not advised as contact dermatitis may result in individuals with sensitive skin and in children.*
3. **Be prepared to treat the victim for shock.** In severe cases, the victim may require hospitalization.
4. If the eyes are stung, irrigate them with at least one quart (1 L) of fresh water or sterile eye wash. **Do not use vinegar in the eyes.** If eye irritation persists, consult an ophthalmologist immediately.

Hydroid and Fire Coral Stings

1. While still underwater, fan seawater over the contact area with your hand without touching the skin. This will help remove some of the nematocysts from the skin's surface. **Do not rub the skin.**
2. Rinse the affected skin with sea water to further remove nematocysts. **Do not rinse with fresh water or apply ice to the affected skin.**
3. Soak the contact area with vinegar until the pain subsides by applying a large gauze pad or piece of cloth (e.g., T-shirt or washcloth) to the skin and dousing it with vinegar. Dry the skin thoroughly. *Note: The use of meat tenderizer is not advised as contact dermatitis may result in individuals with sensitive skin and in children.*
4. Apply a small amount of 1% hydrocortisone lotion to the skin twice daily to reduce itching. Continue treatment until the irritation subsides.
5. If a severe skin rash, itching, swelling or pain persists or an infection develops, contact a physician immediately as antibiotics may be required.

From February to April, warning signs are posted along Florida's east coast swimming beaches to warn bathers of the presence of the Portuguese man-of-war. Photograph by Pat Cunningham.

Man-of-War and Jellyfish Stings
(See next page for box jellyfish stings)

1. **Remove the victim from the water immediately to prevent drowning.**

2. Remove tentacles adhering to the skin by washing the skin with seawater. **Do not wash with fresh water or apply ice and do not rub the affected area.** Rapid removal of the tentacles containing undischarged nematocysts will reduce the total amount of venom that is injected into the victim. **Care should be taken by the rescuers not to touch the tentacles with bare hands.**

3. Rinse the affected area liberally with vinegar. After initially dousing the skin with vinegar, a soft cloth soaked in vinegar may be applied to the contact area for 30 minutes or until pain is alleviated. *Note: The use of meat tenderizer is not advised as contact dermatitis may result in sensitive individuals and in children.*

4. Once the nematocysts have been deactivated (by vinegar), any remaining tentacles may be removed by applying shaving cream and shaving the affected area. After shaving the contact area, reapply vinegar for up to 15 minutes. Remaining tentacles may also be removed with tweezers. Ease the tentacles off the skin in one direction.

5. **Be prepared to treat the victim for shock.** Severe cases may require the administration of artificial respiration or CPR if the pulse and heart beat cease and hospitalization may be required.

6. Standard tetanus prophylaxis and antibiotics may be required for treatment of secondary infections.

Box Jellyfish Stings

1. **Remove the victim from the water immediately to prevent drowning.**

2. For all box jellyfish stings, the use of vinegar is highly recommended in preference to all other treatments. Rinse the affected area liberally with vinegar until pain is alleviated. **Do not wash the affected area with fresh water or rub the affected area.**

3. Rapid removal of tentacles containing undischarged nematocysts will reduce the total amount of venom that is injected into the victim. Remove any remaining tentacles gently with tweezers. Gently ease the tentacles off the skin in one direction. Care should be taken by the rescuers not to touch the tentacles with bare hands.

4. **Be prepared to treat the victim for shock.** Severe cases may require the administration of artificial respiration or CPR if the pulse and heart beat cease and hospitalization may be required.

5. Note: If the victim is stung by an Irukandji stinger, he or she will appear to recover quickly from the mild sting. Warn the victim of the potential general effects (e.g., severe abdominal and chest pain, severe headache, vomiting, and difficulty in breathing) that may ensue within 20 minutes to 2 hours after the sting. Keep the victim calm and give reassurance that the general effects, while painful, are not life-threatening. **Do not allow the victim to return to the water or drive a car.**

6. Standard tetanus prophylaxis and antibiotics may be required for treatment of secondary infections.

7. Box jellyfish antivenom is available for the treatment of envenomations by *Chironex fleckeri* and has proven useful in the treatment of severe stings by other Indo-Pacific box jellyfish species.

Fire Worm Stings

1. Remove the glass-like bristles embedded in the skin using tweezers or by using a piece of adhesive tape to peel them off.

2. Apply vinegar or 40% isopropyl alcohol to the affected skin as soon as possible to reduce the pain. Dry the skin thoroughly.

3. Apply soothing lotion (e.g., calamine lotion) or anesthetic ointment or spray (e.g., benzocaine or lignocaine) to the skin for the first few hours.

4. Apply antibiotic ointment (e.g., neomycin).

5. If pain or swelling persists or if an infection develops, contact a physician immediately as antibiotics may be required.

Cone Stings

1. **Apply a pressure/immobilization bandage as soon as possible to the area of the sting.** (See pages 139–141 for more information). Keep the victim immobilized. Do not remove the pressure/immobilization bandage until the victim is at the hospital.

2. **Cone stings can be life-threatening.** Immediate medical assistance should be sought.

3. Keep the victim calm and give reassurance until medical assistance can be obtained. **Never leave the victim unattended.**

4. In severe cases, paralysis may cause respiratory failure and/or cardiac arrest. **Be prepared to provide artificial respiration or CPR and transport the victim to the hospital as soon as possible.**

Blue-Ringed Octopus Bites
(See below for other Octopus Bites)

1. Immediately wash the wound site with seawater or fresh water to flush venom from the wound.

2. **As soon as possible, apply a pressure/immobilization bandage to the bite area.** (See pages 139–141 for more information). Keep the victim immobilized. Do not remove the pressure/immobilization bandage until the victim is at the hospital.

3. **The bite of several species of blue-ringed octopus can be life-threatening.** Immediate medical assistance should be sought.

4. Keep the victim calm and give reassurance until medical assistance can be obtained. **Never leave the victim unattended.**

5. In severe cases, paralysis may cause respiratory failure and/or cardiac arrest. **Be prepared to provide artificial respiration and CPR, and transport the victim to the hospital as soon as possible.**

Octopus Bites

1. Immediately wash the wound site with seawater or fresh water to flush venom from the wound.

2. The bite of most octopus species is generally not life-threatening.

3. Keep the victim calm and give reassurance until medical assistance can be obtained. **Never leave the victim unattended.**

4. In severe cases, breathing difficulties may develop. **Be prepared to provide artificial respiration and CPR, and transport the victim to the hospital as soon as possible.**

Sea Cucumber Contacts

1. After handling a sea cucumber, wash the area of contact with sea water. Never rub the affected hands across the face or eyes.

2. Apply a large gauze pad or piece of cloth to the skin and douse it with vinegar until the pain subsides. If vinegar is unavailable, 40% isopropyl alcohol may be substituted. Dry the skin thoroughly.

3. If the eyes are irritated by the mucus, irrigate them immediately with at least one quart (1 L) of fresh water or sterile eye wash. **Do not use vinegar or alcohol in the eyes.** If eye irritation persists, consult an ophthalmologist immediately.

At various bathing beaches along the Queensland Coast, first aid stations have been erected containing a gallon of vinegar for dousing box jellyfish stings. Photograph by Paul Goetz.

Crown of Thorns Sea Star Envenomations

1. Remove any loose pieces of the spines with tweezers trying not to break off the spines under the skin. The spines should be pulled out straight, and not bent, because they can break off at the tips.

2. Do not crush a spine already embedded under the skin because this will make it impossible to remove. **Deeply embedded spines, particularly those around joints, nerves, or blood vessels should be surgically removed.**

3. Bathe the wound in hot water to tolerance (115°F or 45°C) for up to 90 minutes. The rescuer should test the water temperature to ensure it will not burn the victim. If hot water is not available, use chemical hotpacks around the wound site. (**See Cautionary Note on page 135.**) Repeat the heat therapy if the pain recurs.

4. Once pain relief has been achieved, the affected limb should be immobilized in an elevated position.

5. The victim should be transported immediately to a hospital where a physician can clean, disinfect, and suture the wound. Antibiotics are often required for treatment of secondary infections. An X ray should be taken to determine the presence of any remaining spine fragments.

6. Tetanus prophylaxis is advisable for the deep puncture-type wounds produced by the spines.

During the 1970s, warning signs were posted in Florida and the Caribbean at swimming beaches where long-spined sea urchins were abundant. Photograph by Pat Cunningham.

Sea Urchin Spine or Pedicellaria Envenomations

1. Remove any visible pieces of the spines with tweezers trying not to break off the spines under the skin.

2. Do not crush a spine already embedded under the skin because this will make it impossible to remove. **Deeply embedded spines, particularly around joints, nerves, or blood vessels, should be surgically removed.**

3. If the victim has been envenomated by pedicellariae (minute three-jawed pincers), remove the pedicellariae immediately with tweezers or apply shaving cream to the wound site and gently shave the area. Pedicellariae must be removed or venom will continue to be released into the wound.

4. Bathe the wound in hot water (115°F or 45°C) for up to 90 minutes to reduce pain. The rescuer should test the water temperature to ensure it will not burn the victim. If hot water is not available, use chemical hotpacks around the wound site. (**See Cautionary Note on page 135.**) Repeat the heat therapy if the pain recurs.

5. Apply antiseptic (e.g., betadine or iodine) and a local anesthetic (e.g., benzocaine) spray or ointment to the wound site.

6. **Be prepared to treat the victim for shock.** In severe cases, respiratory failure and/or cardiac arrest may occur. Be prepared to provide artificial respiration or CPR, and transport the victim to the hospital as soon as possible.

7. If pain or swelling of the wound persists, contact a physician immediately as antibiotics may be required.

8. Tetanus prophylaxis is advisable for the deep puncture-type wounds produced by the spines.

Stingray and Venomous Fish Stings

1. Wash the wound immediately with seawater or fresh water to flush the venom from the wound.

2. Bathe the wound in hot water to tolerance (115°F or 45°C) for up to 90 minutes. The rescuer should test the water temperature to ensure it will not burn the victim. If hot water is not available, use chemical hotpacks around the wound site. (**See Cautionary Note on page 135.**) Repeat the heat therapy if the pain recurs.

3. Gently remove the stinger or spines and any associated tissue from the wound. Once pain relief has been achieved, the affected limb should be immobilized in an elevated position.

The sharp dorsal spines of some scorpionfish are well camouflaged with ragged skin flaps. Photograph by Pat Cunningham.

4. The victim should be transported to a hospital where a physician can clean, disinfect, and suture the wound. Antibiotics are often required for treatment of secondary infections.

5. Tetanus prophylaxis is advisable for the deep laceration-type or puncture-type wounds produced by stingrays and other fish envenomations.

6. Note: If the envenomation was produced by a stonefish, stonefish antivenom may be used once identification of the sting is confirmed. Currently, antivenoms are not available for treatment of stingray or any other venomous fish stings.

Sea Snake Bites

1. Do not use incision and/or suction methods (e.g., snake bite kits) to remove venom unless they can be used immediately after the bite.

2. **Apply a pressure/immobilization bandage immediately to the bite area** (See pages 139–141 for more information). Do not remove the pressure/immobilization bandage until the victim is at the hospital.

3. **Reassure the victim and keep the victim calm and as immobilized as possible.** Note: Any movement by the victim will only

accelerate circulation and absorption of the venom from the bite site to other parts of the body.

4. **Seek medical assistance immediately.** The victim should be transported to a hospital for clinical evaluation as soon as possible after the bite. Sea snake antivenom is available and is highly effective in reducing recovery time and the general effects produced by the venom.

5. If the sea snake that bit the victim was captured and killed, bring it to the hospital for identification. However, rescuers should not endanger themselves by trying to collect the offending sea snake.

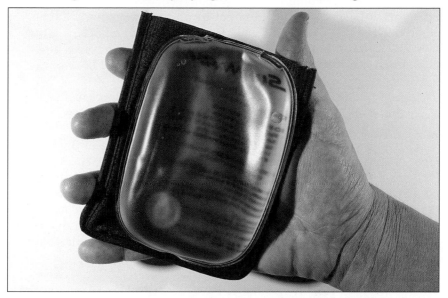

Chemical hotpacks can be carried in the first aid kit as an instant substitute for hot water immersion therapy for stingray and other venomous fish stings. Photograph by Paul

Cautionary Note

Several brands of chemical hotpacks attain temperatures exceeding 125°F (51°C) immediately after being activated. These temperatures may burn sensitive skin areas, particularly in children and the elderly. Rescuers should use caution and wrap the hotpack in a soft cloth during the first few minutes of use. Most chemical hotpacks maintain a temperature of 115°F (45°C) or more for 30 minutes.

Basic First Aid Kit

Although it may not always be practical to carry all of the items in a basic first aid kit, anyone who spends a great deal of time around the marine environment should try to have most of these items readily available in the event an emergency occurs. Enrollment in a basic first aid and CPR course given by the Red Cross or other health agency will provide experience in responding to medical emergencies. Additionally, tetanus immunizations should be kept current by all those who enjoy the marine environment.

Many SCUBA diving clubs assign one member to prepare a club first aid kit that can be carried to all sponsored dive outings. In this way, all members are protected for a small individual cost.

A more complete first aid kit, useful in areas where immediate medical treatment is unavailable, is described by Auerbach and Halstead in *Management of Wilderness and Environmental Emergencies.*

All boat owners, especially those who conduct fishing or diving charters, should have a basic first aid kit on board for their passengers' safety. If divers are the primary passengers, this should include an adequate supply of emergency oxygen and the knowledge to administer it properly. For dive boats, the Divers Alert Network (DAN) defines an adequate oxygen supply as an amount sufficient to manage at least one buddy pair of injured divers until they can be transferred to an Emergency Medical System (EMS).

REMEMBER: Two Important Rules of First Aid Treatment

1. On-site first aid treatment of envenomations is intended to supplement and not substitute for professional medical treatment by a physician.
2. **Never underestimate the effect of an envenomation** and be prepared to seek immediate medical attention for the victim if required.

Contents of a Basic First Aid Kit

To obtain emergency assistance:
  LIST OF EMERGENCY TELEPHONE NUMBERS
  TAPE COINS FOR PHONE TO INSIDE COVER OF KIT

To denature and to flush venom from the wound:
  VINEGAR
  40% ISOPROPYL ALCOHOL
  STERILE EYE WASH SOLUTION
  CHEMICAL HOTPACKS (**See Cautionary Note on page 135**)

To remove spines, nematocysts, or stinger from the wound:
  ADHESIVE TAPE
  TWEEZERS
  SHAVING CREAM and RAZOR

To disinfect wound:
  BETADINE SOLUTION
  HYDROGEN PEROXIDE SOLUTION
  NEOMYCIN OINTMENT
  BACITRACIN OINTMENT

To relieve pain and itching:
  CALAMINE LOTION
  CORTISONE or HYDROCORTISONE CREAM
  ASPIRIN
  BENZOCAINE or LIGNOCAINE SPRAY

For allergic reactions:
  BENADRYL CAPSULES (25 mg)

To treat shock:
  SPACE BLANKET
  OXYGEN BOTTLE

Instructions for emergency first aid procedures:
  CPR (CARDIOPULMONARY RESUSCITATION)
  ADMINISTRATION OF OXYGEN
  SHOCK
  PRESSURE/IMMOBILIZATION TECHNIQUE

Emergency Telephone Numbers

LOCAL EMERGENCY ASSISTANCE IN THE UNITED STATES

Dial 911 for Rescue Squad/Ambulance Service

Dial 0 for OPERATOR to direct call to Emergency Services

Print telephone numbers for local emergency medical services below:

EMERGENCY ASSISTANCE WORLDWIDE

The **Divers Alert Network (DAN)** is a nonprofit organization that provides medical information and advice to the diving public, supports diving research, and maintains a 24-hour emergency telephone line for diving-related accidents including marine envenomations. Contact DAN Headquarters, Duke University, Durham, NC, (919) 684-2948 for further information. For serious accidents—your first call should be to local emergency medical services.

DAN USA EMERGENCIES (919) 684-8111

DAN USA DIVING MEDICAL INFORMATION LINE
(919) 684-2948, ext. 222
(Available Monday through Friday, 9 a.m. to 5 p.m. EST)

DAN AUSTRALASIA (DES) EMERGENCIES
1-800-088-200 (within Australia)

DAN AUSTRALASIA (DES) EMERGENCIES
61-8-373-5312 (from outside Australia)

MARINE STINGER 24 HOUR REPORTING LINE (008) (015160)
(For medical advice for box jellyfish stings within Australia)

DAN EUROPE EMERGENCIES 41-1-383-1111

DAN JAPAN EMERGENCIES 81-3-3812-4999

DAN JAPAN MEDICAL INFORMATION LINE 81-3-3590-6501

Pressure/Immobilization Technique

The pressure/immobilization technique is currently recommended for treatment of three types of marine envenomations: sea snake bites, blue-ringed octopus bites, and cone stings. This technique consists of the application of a broad pressure-bearing bandage over the wound site, and subsequent immobilization of the affected limb using splints and additional bandages or a sling. Pressure/immobilization bandages should be applied with the same pressure that would be used to treat a sprained wrist or ankle. The bandages must never be applied so tightly as to become a tourniquet that inhibits normal circulation. The victim's fingers or toes on the affected limb should be checked to ensure that there is no loss in sensation and that the extremity remains pink in color. **Once applied, it is of utmost importance that the pressure/immobilization bandage remains in place until the victim arrives at a medical facility.** Premature removal of the bandage may cause life-threatening results as venom from the immobilized limb can then enter the blood stream and further circulate to other more vulnerable areas of the body. The pressure/immobilization bandage may remain in place for up to 24 hours.

Apply a gauze pad to the wound site and begin wrapping a cloth or elastic bandage around affected limb. Photograph by Paul Goetz.

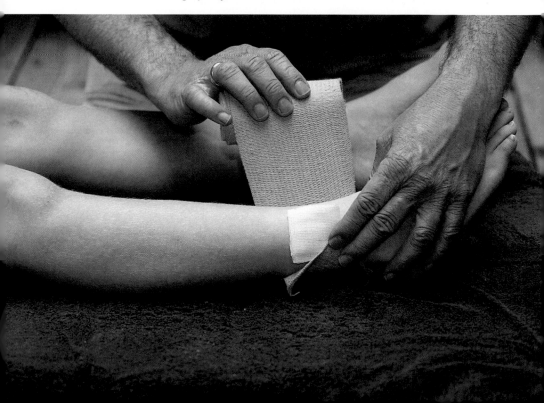

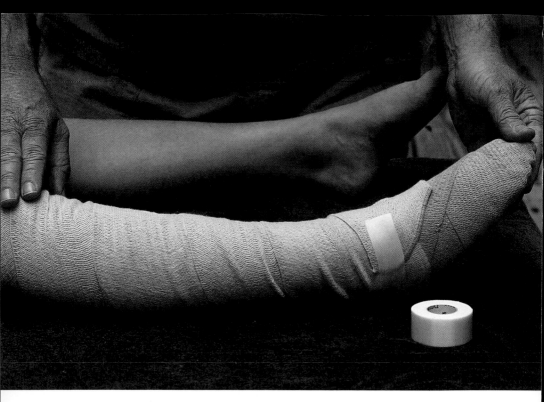

Wrap the limb area adjoining the wound site and especially the proximal portion of the limb. Photograph by Paul Goetz.

After wrapping the limb, a splint should be applied with additional bandages to further immobilize the limb. The victim should be kept calm, as immobile as possible, and reassured. Photograph by Paul Goetz.

The following steps should be taken to apply a pressure/immobilization bandage:

1. Place several 3 × 3 inch square (7.5 × 7.5 cm) gauze pads directly on the wound area.

2. While holding the gauze pads in place, begin applying a broad pressure-bearing elastic or cloth bandage over the site of the envenomation and as much of the adjoining part of the limb as possible especially the proximal portion nearest the torso.

3. After the bandage is in place, the limb should be immobilized further by applying a splint and wrapping it with additional elastic bandages, cloth bandages, or adhesive tape.

4. The victim should be kept calm, remain as immobile as possible, and be reassured repeatedly by rescuers.

5. For hand or arm envenomations, the pressure/immobilization bandage should be applied from the hand to the elbow, and then a splint applied to the elbow. A sling also may be used to hold the arm immobile across the chest.

6. For envenomations to areas such as the torso and neck where application of a pressure/immobilization bandage would be impossible, sustained pressure using a folded cloth or gauze pads can be applied to the wound site by the weight of the victim's body or by a rescuer's hand.

7. The victim should be transported as quickly as possible to the nearest hospital.

Glossary

Anterior. Pertaining to the head or front end.

Aperture. The round or elliptical shaped opening at the end of the body whorl of a snail shell into which the mollusk can withdraw.

Basal. Of, at, or forming the base of an organism.

Benthic. Of, or pertaining to, organisms that live in or on the sea bottom in sediment or on hard substrate.

Body whorl. The last and usually the largest turn or whorl in the spiral shell of a gastropod snail.

Calcareous. Containing calcium carbonate and usually related to structures that are hardened such as bones, shells, or plates.

Cartilage. Connective tissue composed of cellular material surrounded by tough, flexible protein fibers. The skeletons of all chondrichthyes such as sharks, skates, and stingrays are composed entirely of cartilage.

Circumtropical. Organisms distributed in warm tropical ocean waters worldwide.

Cnidocyte. A specialized cell containing a nematocyst or stinging cell that is most abundant on the surface of the tentacles and mouth parts of Cnidarians.

Colonial. Of, or living in a colony or colonies.

Commensal. A symbiotic relationship between two different species in which each exists without causing obvious harm or benefit to the other.

CPR. Cardiopulmonary resuscitation.

Cryptic. Hidden or concealing.

Denature. To change the physical structure of a molecule and thereby alter its chemical and biological activity.

Dermatitis. Inflammation of the skin.

Diurnal. Active during the day.

Dorsal. Pertaining to the upper surface of an organism that is generally not in contact with the bottom sediments.

Envenomation. To introduce venom from one organism into another.

Estuary. Area where fresh river water intermixes with seawater.

Gonads. Sex glands or organs; ovaries in females and testes in males.

Habitat. The living environment in which an organism is found.

Herbivore. An animal that feeds exclusively on plants.

Intertidal. The area intermittently covered by water between the high tide mark and the low tide mark.

Laceration. A wound with a torn, jagged, or mangled edge.

Larva. An early developmental stage of any animal that changes structurally as it becomes an adult. (larvae pl.)

Madreporite. The porous plate on the dorsal surface of an echinoderm through which the internal water vascular system opens to the exterior.

Margin. The edge of the bell of a medusa.

Medusa. One of two body forms that may occur in Cnidarians. A free-swimming bell-shaped form characteristic of jellyfish that propels itself through the water by rhythmic muscular contractions. (medusae pl.)

Multicellular. An organism composed of many cells.

Nematocyst. A specialized stinging cell usually located on the tentacles or mouth parts of Cnidarians containing an explosive capsule that discharges a stinging or entangling thread when stimulated.

Nocturnal. Active during the night.

Oral disc. The flat upper surface of sea anemones and polyps containing a mouth surrounded by tentacles.

Ossicles. Small calcareous plates that form the internal skeleton or test of some Echinoderms.

Papilla. Any small cone-shaped protuberance on the body wall.

Parapodia. Paired appendages on each body segment of polychaete worms. (parapodium sing.)

Pectoral fin. The paired fins attached to the shoulder girdle of a fish.

Pedicellaria. A small pincer-like structure on the body surface of sea stars and sea urchins. (pedicellariae pl.)

Pelagic. Pertaining to organisms that live in the open ocean.

Pelvic fin. The paired fins on the lower part of a fish's body, just below or behind the pectoral fins.

Phylum. Any of the major taxonomic divisions of the plant and animal kingdom. A phylum is further divided into classes. (Phyla pl.)

Pinnate. Branched in a feather-like pattern.

Planktonic. Small organisms that drift in the upper surface layers of the ocean and are carried by currents. Phytoplankton are planktonic plants, while zooplankton are planktonic animals.

Polyp. One of two body forms that may occur in Cnidarians. This is a sedentary cylindrical-shaped form (e.g., coral and sea anemones) with a mouth surrounded by tentacles at one end and with the other end attached to the substrate.

Posterior. Pertaining to the rear or anal end of an organism.

Proboscis. An extensible and flexible head structure commonly associated with the mouth in gastropods that is used in feeding.

Radially symmetric. A type of body structure that radiates out into all directions from a central point.

Radula. A ribbon-shaped membrane attached to the floor of the buccal cavity in gastropod snails to which many small hard teeth are attached in transverse rows. In cones, the radula is modified into a harpoon-shaped venomous tooth.

Rays. One of two supporting elements in the fin membranes of fishes that are either flexible (rays) or stiff (spines).

Sedentary. Pertaining to animals that are either attached to the substrate or that are unattached but that do not move.

Setae. Bristle-like structures located on each body segment of polychaete worms. These hollow glass-like bristles break off on contact.

Siliceous. Composed of silica.

Spicule. A small siliceous or calcareous supporting structure that may be needle-like, dart-like, or jack-like in appearance and found in the body tissues of soft coral and sponges.

Spines. One of two supporting elements in the fin membranes of fishes that are either stiff (spines) or flexible (rays). Also any of the sharp, stiff projections on sting rays or invertebrates (e.g., sea urchins).

Spongin. Fibrous organic skeletal material found in some sponges.

Substrate. The medium upon which an organism grows.

Subtidal. The area of coastal waters that is below the low tide mark.

Symbiotic. An intimate relationship between two species, that may be described either as (1) *parasitism,* in which one species benefits at the expense of the host species, (2) *commensalism,* in which the two species exist together without obvious benefit or harm to each other, or (3) *mutualism,* in which both species appear to benefit from the relationship.

Test. The hard outer covering composed of fused calcareous plates that forms the bodies of sea urchins.

Tube feet. Small tubular projections often tipped with suction discs forming part of the water vascular system in echinoderms that are used in locomotion, feeding, and sensory functions.

Ventral. Pertaining to the lower surface of an organism that is typically in contact with the sediment.

Virulent. Highly injurious or deadly; producing a rapid, violent reaction.

Visceral mass. The major body mass of cephalopods (octopus) containing the digestive, reproductive, excretory, and respiratory systems.

Water vascular system. The hydraulic system of canals that operates the contraction or extension of the tube feet of Echinoderms.

Windward. The direction or side from which the wind blows.

Zooanthellae. Photosynthesizing one-celled plants that live symbiotically inside the tissues of various invertebrates (e.g., hard coral and jellyfish).

Bibliography

Abbott, R. T. *American Seashells—The Marine Mollusca of the Atlantic and Pacific Coasts of North America.* New York: Van Nostrand Reinhold Company, 1974.

Allen, G. R. and Steene, R. *Indo-Pacific Coral Reef Field Guide.* Singapore: Tropical Reef Research, 1994.

Auerbach, P. S. *A Medical Guide to Hazardous Marine Life.* St. Louis: Mosby-Year Book Inc., 1991.

Auerbach, P. S. and Halstead, B. W. "Hazardous Marine Life." pp. 213–259. In: Auerbach, P. S. and Geehr, E. C. (Editors). *Management of Wilderness and Environmental Emergencies.* New York: Macmillian Publishing Company, 1983.

Auerbach, P. S. and Halstead, B. 1982. "Marine Hazards: Attacks and Envenomations," *Journal of Emergency Nursing* 8 (3), pp. 115–122.

Barnes, R. D. *Invertebrate Zoology,* Fourth Edition. Philadelphia: Holt, Rinehart and Winston, 1980.

Bookspan, J. "Things That Sting." *Alert Diver,* January–February, pp. 18–20, 1994.

Boschung, H. T., Williams, J. D., Gotshall, D. W., Caldwell, D. K. and Caldwell, M. C. *The Audubon Society Field Guide to North American Fishes, Whales and Dolphins.* New York: Chanticleer Press, Alfred A. Knopf Publishers, 1983.

Burnett, J. W. "Jellyfish Envenomations—Treating the Sting." *Alert Diver,* January–February, pp. 22, 1994.

Coleman, N. *Hazardous Sea Creatures—A Personal Survival Guide.* Rochedale, Australia: Sea Australia Resource Center, 1993.

Coleman, N. *Encyclopedia of Marine Animals.* Pymble, Australia: Collins Angus and Robertson Publishers Pty. Limited, 1991.

Divers Alert Network (DAN) at Duke University Medical Center, Durham, NC. "Case History File 0481-0016A." *Alert Diver 1* (4):10, 1985.

Drayton, G. E. Aquatic Skin Disorders. pp. 260–269. In: Auerbach, P. S. and Geehr, E. C. (Ed). *Management of Wilderness and Environmental Emergencies.* New York: Macmillian Publishing Company, 1983.

Dunn, D. F. "Menacing Medusae, Horrible Hydroids, and Noxious Cnidarians." *Oceans* (2), pp. 16–23, 1982.

Dunson, W. A. *The Biology of Sea Snakes.* Baltimore: University Park Press, 1975.

Edmonds, C. *Dangerous Marine Animals*. Frenchs Forest, Australia, Reed Books Pty. Ltd., 1989.

Exton, D. (Editor). *The Marine Stinger Book, Third Edition*. Brisbane, Australia: The Surf Life Saving Association of Australia. Queensland State Centre, Inc., 1985.

Fisher, A. A. *Atlas of Aquatic Dermatology*. New York: Grune and Stratton, 1978.

Freiberg, M. and Wall, J. G. *The World of Venomous Marine Animals*. Neptune City, NJ: T.F.H. Publications, Inc., 1984.

George, J. D. and George, J. J. *Marine Life—An Illustrated Encyclopedia of Invertebrates in the Sea*. New York: Wiley-Interscience, John Wiley and Sons, 1979.

Gotshall D. W. *Marine Animals of Baja California: A Guide to the Common Fishes and Invertebrates, 2nd Ed*. Monterey, CA: Sea Challenges, 1987.

Gotshall, D. W. *Pacific Coast Inshore Fishes, Third Edition*. Monterey, CA: Sea Challengers, 1989.

Gow, G. *Graeme Gow's Complete Guide to Australian Snakes*. North Ryde, Australia: Angus and Robertson Publishers, 1989.

Habermehl, G. G. *Venomous Animals and Their Toxins*. Berlin, Germany: Springer-Verlag. Berlin, 1981.

Halstead, B. W. *Dangerous Aquatic Animals of the World.: A Color Atlas*. Princeton: The Darwin Press Inc., 1992.

Halstead, B. W. *Dangerous Marine Animals*. Centerville, MD: Cornell Maritime Press, 1980.

Humann, P. *Reef Coral Identification—Florida, Caribbean and Bahamas*. Jacksonville, FL: New World Publications, Inc., 1993.

Humann, P. *Reef Fish Identification—Galapagos*. Jacksonville, FL: New World Publications, 1993.

Humann, P. *Reef Creature Identification—Florida, Caribbean, and Bahamas*. Jacksonville, FL: New World Publications, 1992.

Humann, P. *Reef Fish Identification—Florida, Caribbean, and Bahamas*. Jacksonville, FL: New World Publications, 1989.

Kaplan, E. H. *A Field Guide to Coral Reefs of the Caribbean and Florida Including Bermuda and the Bahamas*. (A Peterson Field Guide Series). Boston: Houghton Mifflin Company, 1982.

Kay, E. A. *Hawaiian Marine Shells—Reef and Shore Fauna of Hawaii. Volume 4 Mollusca*. Honolulu: Bishop Museum Press, 1977.

Kuiter, R. H. *Coastal Fishes of South-Eastern Australia*. Honolulu: University of Hawaii Press, 1993.

Lythgoe, J. and Lythgoe, G. *Fishes of the Sea. The North Atlantic and Mediterranean*. Cambridge, The MIT Press, 1992.

Marsh, J. A. *Cone Shells of the World.* Brisbane, Australia: Jacaranda Press, 1974.

Marsh, L. M. and Slack-Smith, S. M. *Sea Stingers.* Western Australian Museum, Perth, Australia, 1986.

Martinez, A. J. *Marine Life of the North Atlantic—Canada to New England.* Wenham, MA: Marine Life, 1994.

Mebane, G. Y. "Spines." *Alert Diver,* January–February, pp. 32–37, 1995.

Meinkoth, N. A. *The Audubon Society Field Guide to North American Seashore Creatures.* New York: Chanticleer Press, Alfred A. Knopf Publishers, 1981.

Michael, S. W. *Reef Sharks and Rays of the World — A Guide to their Identification, Behavior, and Ecology.* Monterey, CA.: Sea Challengers, 1993.

Nelson, J. S. *Fishes of the World.* New York: John Wiley and Sons Inc., 1994.

Randall, J. E., G. R. Allen and R. C. Steene. *Fishes of the Great Barrier Reef and Coral Sea.* Bathurst, Australia: Crawford House Press, 1990.

Randall, J. E. *Caribbean Reef Fishes.* Neptune City, NJ: T.F.H. Publications, Inc., 1968.

Reader's Digest. *Reader's Digest Book of the Great Barrier Reef.* Sidney, Australia: Reader's Digest Services, 1984.

Russell, F. E. *Marine Toxins and Venomous and Poisonous Marine Animals.* London: Academic Press, Inc., 1965.

Sefton, N. and Webster, S. *Caribbean Reef Invertebrates.* Monterey, CA: Sea Challengers, 1986.

Schwartz, F. *Common Jellyfish and Comb Jellies of North Carolina.* Morehead City, NC: University of North Carolina, Institute of Marine Science, 1979.

Shirai, S. *Ecological Encyclopedia of the Marine Animals of the Indo-Pacific. Volume 1—Vertebrata.* Tokyo: Shin Nippon Kyoiku Tosho Company, 1986.

Solem, G. A. *The Shell Makers—Introducing Mollusks.* New York: Wiley-Interscience, John Wiley and Sons, 1974.

Stokes, F. J. *Hand Guide to the Coral Reef Fishes of the Caribbean and Adjacent Tropical Waters including Florida, Bermuda, and the Bahamas.* New York: Lippincott and Crowell, 1980.

Sutty, L. *Seashell Treasures of the Caribbean.* New York: E. P. Dutton Inc., 1986.

Veron, J. E. N. *Corals of Australia and the Indo-Pacific.* Honolulu: University of Hawaii Press, 1993.

Zeiller, W. *Tropical Marine Invertebrates of Southern Florida and the Bahama Islands.* New York: Wiley-Interscience. John Wiley and Sons, 1974.

Index

Boldface page numbers indicate photographs.